A COMPANION TO THE
LITURGY

A GUIDE TO WORSHIP IN
THE REFORMED CHURCH IN AMERICA

GARRETT C. ROORDA
EDITOR

THE HALF MOON PRESS
NEW YORK

TABLE OF CONTENTS

		Page
Introduction	Richard C. Oudersluys	V
Chapter I	Worship and Liturgy in the Reformed Church	1
	Garrett C. Roorda	
Chapter II	The Order of Worship	12
	Garrett C. Roorda	
Chapter III	The Orders for the Sacrament of Baptism	22
	James C. Eelman	
Chapter IV	The Order for the Sacrament of the Lord's Supper	35
	Howard G. Hageman	
Chapter V	Liturgy and Music	44
	Laurence Grooters	
Chapter VI	Liturgy and Ceremonial	51
	Charles W. Krahe, Jr.	
Chapter VII	Liturgy and Architecture	57
	Donald J. Bruggink	
Chapter VIII	The Marriage Service	65
	Garrett C. Roorda	

INTRODUCTION:

The Making of Our Revised Liturgy and It's Commentary

Perhaps it is important to explain what is implied in the appearance of this companion volume to our *Liturgy and Psalms* which was published and presented to the General Synod of 1968. The Synod of that year charged the Permanent Committee on Liturgy to prepare and publish a *Companion to the Liturgy*, which would be useful for ministers in conducting the various services of worship, and also for the better understanding of the Liturgy by the church in general. This book is the committee's response to that recent commission. It is in fact, a series of essays which aim to provide a theological and practical commentary on the Liturgy itself, and the worship and liturgical practice of the Reformed Church in America. The publication of this companion handbook also implies some history. The close sequence of these two publications prompts the committee to hope that it may be helpful to place them in some kind of historical perspective.

The recent revision of our Liturgy was the culmination of eighteen years of work, undertaken originally at the direction of the General Synod of 1950, and entrusted to an unusually small Committee on Revision of the Liturgy consisting of four persons.[1] This committee was constituted with the stipulation that it proceed to the revision of the Liturgy of 1906, a provision which, incidentally, was not always remembered by the church at large or its lower assemblies. In order to clarify their task for themselves and the church, the committee published a series of preliminary studies in which they outlined briefly our liturgical history together with brief sketches of the principles and the scope of the revisional task as it was then envisioned.[2] In 1952

[1]The Committee appointed consisted of M. Stephen James, Chairman, Howard G. Hageman, Richard C. Oudersluys, and Gerrit T. Vander Lugt.

[2]The studies which served as working papers for the Committee were published in the Church Herald, four in number: "Our Liturgical History," by Howard G. Hageman, May 4, 1951; "Principles of Reformed Worship," by Gerrit T. Vander Lugt, May 11, 1951; "The Place and Need for a Formulated Liturgy in the Reformed Church," by Richard C. Oudersluys, May 18, 1951; and "The Needed Scope of Liturgical Revision," by M. Stephen James, May 25, 1951.

the committee was able to present to Synod the first of a series of revised texts for all of the obligatory forms, and with them a request that they be made available to the church for provisional use and evaluation. It was also requested that the committee be enlarged by the addition of one member from Particular Synods not represented in its membership, in order to facilitate a more church-wide evaluation and expression. The Synod authorized permissive use of the revisions by the church for a period of three years. The forms were printed and distributed in 1953, and in the following year the Synod enlarged the committee as previously requested.[3] Evaluations and responses from classes and individual churches were not numerous, but heeding and incorporating such suggestions as had been received, the committee submitted to the Synod of 1955 a new set of revised texts for the obligatory forms, asking this time that they be remanded to the classes for approval. The committee also reported continuing work on the numerous optional forms, the lectionary, and the treasury of prayers.

In the light of subsequent events, the request of the committee for approval of the revised forms by the classes was ill-advised. It became apparent at once that the church at large had not kept pace with the work of the committee. Faced by the need to make a decision respecting the revisional work of the committee, the classes only now began their own work of serious liturgical education and study. With necessity upon them, committees were appointed, and they met, discussed, studied and reported, but the time factor was to prove decisive. While it may be possible for some Protestants to change their liturgy or theology easily and quickly, it is not so with cautious minded, slow moving Calvinists, and requesting them to approve a revised liturgy within five years was expecting too much, too soon. It was not surprising, therefore, that the classes registered with the General Synod of 1956 a bewildering set of annotated votes of approval and disapproval. The disapproving votes were so

[3]The Particular Synod representatives added to the Committee were Theodore Luidens (Albany Synod), Garrett C. Roorda (New York Synod), and John S. Ter Louw (Chicago Synod). The New Jersey Synod was already represented by Howard G. Hageman, and the Iowa Synod by Gerrit T. Vander Lugt. The later division of the Chicago Synod into the two Synods of Chicago and Michigan brought into the Committee Bert E. Van Soest as the Chicago Synod representative.

diversely negative that their proper interpretation was given over
to a special Committee on Reactions to the Revision of the
Liturgy, with instruction to report their recommendations before
the close of synod. Desirous of conserving five years of revisional
work, and sensitive to the predicament of the church at large,
the special committee bridged the crisis situation with a series
of constructive recommendations: that the Committee on Revision
of the Liturgy continue its work, that the committee communicate with the classes respecting their responses to the proposed
revisions, and that the period of permissive use be extended for
another year.[4]

Fully aware that it needed to moderate the pace of revisional
work, the committee used the year of 1957 to set out a course
of liturgical education and promotion. Continuing to work on its
own unfinished agenda, the committee now entered upon ex-
tensive correspondence with individuals, consistories and classes,
eliciting criticisms, answering objections, adjusting contradictory
counsels and recommendations.

Utilizing as much as possible this church-wide expression on
liturgy, the committee submitted to the Synod of 1958 the third
in its series of revised texts, requesting that they be sent to the
classes for provisional use and study over a period not to exceed
five years. The Synod authorized this course of action, and it
proved to be the better part of wisdom. In 1959 the committee
reported the need for a fourth printing of the Provisional Liturgy,
some 15,500 copies having been distributed for experimental use
and study. At the same synod, specimen texts for the optional
forms were submitted and immediately approved.[5] During the
ensuing five years, diligent effort was made to keep open

[4]The members of this special Committee were as follows: Ministers,
Norman Thomas, Willard Meengs, Harold Englund; Elders, John E.
Muller, Robert Wardlow.
[5]The optional forms included orders for the Solemnization of Marriage, for
the Visitation of the Sick, the Dying, for the Organization of a New
Congregation, for the Laying of the Cornerstone of a Church Building, for
the Dedication of a Church, for the Dedication of Memorials, Gifts and
Furnishings. The texts were incorporated in the Minutes of the General
Synod of 1959 (325-345). In 1961 orders of service for the Burial of the
Dead were submitted and printed in full in the Minutes of the General
Synod of 1961 (369-377). Small editorial additions and changes con-
tinued to be made in the optional forms until the time of final publication,
reporting the same annually to General Synod and receiving authorization.

the lines of communication between the committee and the classes. The committee wrote articles in the Church Herald, published annual progress reports to the General Synod, provided leadership for numerous workshops on liturgy and worship, responded to overtures from various church assemblies, and pushed to completion work on the lectionary, the new disposition of the Psalms and canticles arranged according to the calendar of the Christian year, and the treasury of prayers. During those busy years, the personnel of the committee membership underwent many changes, and a debt of graditude is owing to those who shared both the burden and the joy of heavy study and writing assignments.[6] In 1965 the final series of revised texts for the obligatory forms were presented to Synod and sent to the classes for approval, and in 1966 the Synod passed a declaratory act of approval, authorizing at the same time their publication along with the older forms of 1906. The following year Synod authorized the inclusion of the Standards of Unity of the Reformed Churches, all of them appearing in new translations.[7] The year was spent largely in preparing the typescript of the new publication and in proof-reading, the burden of which was carried by the chairman, Gerrit T. Vander Lugt. At the official presentation of the new *Liturgy and Psalms* to the General Synod of 1968, it had been planned to present a specially inscribed copy to Dr. Vander Lugt as a token of gratitude for his uninterrupted work of eighteen years, but divine providence intervened. Dr. Vander Lugt died on May 1, 1968, as the last pages of the book made their way through the press.

[6]It is perhaps appropriate to list the membership of the Committee changes through the years: M. Stephen James (1950-1959), Howard G. Hageman (1950-1966), Richard C. Oudersluys (1950-1970), Gerrit T. Vander Lugt (1950-1968), Theodore Luidens (1955-1965), Garrett C. Roorda (1954-1965), 1967-1970), John S. Ter Louw (1954-1959), Bert E. Van Soest (1959-1962), Harold Schadewald (1959-1969), Arvin Roos (1960-1964), Russell Vande Bunte (1960-1967), Glen O. Peterman (1963-1968), Gordon Girod (1964-1967), Charles Krahe, Jr., (1965-1971), Laurence Grooters (1965-1971), Donald R. Wing (1967-1972), Donald Bruggink (1966-1969), James Eelman (1968-1971), Robert Wildman (1967-1970), William Brownson (1969-1972).

[7]*The Heidelberg Catechism* is given in the translation of Allen O. Miller and M. Eugene Osterhaven, Copyright 1962, and used with their permission; the *Belgic Confession* and the *Canons of the Synod of Dordt* are given in the translation of Gerrit T. Vander Lugt and used by his permission.

It was fitting that the prepared inscribed copy together with a tribute from a grateful church were presented instead to his beloved wife who had shared with him the work of the years. Whatever may or may not be claimed for the *Liturgy and Psalms*, it can at least be said that it was the work of the many as well as the few. This is as it should be, since liturgy is the work of the people of God.

Although preparatory work on a companion manual to the Liturgy had been in progress for some time, the Synod of 1968 now authorized the Permanent Committee on Liturgy to proceed with its completion and publication. Under the editorship of Garrett C. Roorda, the present chairman of the committee, the book is now at hand. The chapters illustrate the indisputable alternation between theology and liturgy. Liturgy constantly recalls theology to its pastoral task, and theology knows that it comes alive only when the worshipper encounters the living God in the Word and the Sacraments. And since our symbols are not verbal only, and worship involves not only what the preacher says but what the worshipper does, we need to concern ourselves, especially in these times, with all the symbols of the church — architecture, music, ceremonies and ornament. What is put forward here is not intended to fetter freedom or infringe on reliance upon the Holy Spirit, but simply to assist us in making dignified, meaningful and reverent the conduct of worship according to our Reformed heritage and usage. This book is offered to the church with the hope that it may help in making divine worship come alive in the life of each succeeding generation.

— Richard C. Oudersluys

Chapter I

WORSHIP AND LITURGY IN THE REFORMED CHURCH IN AMERICA

"Her Mode of Worship is expressed in the Liturgy...." With these words the General Synod of the Reformed Church in America introduced the first American edition of the Constitution in 1793. The passage of time has not altered the essential truth stated in these words. Many things have changed, but the essence of worship, shaped by the holy Scriptures and the history of the people of God, remains the same. Such things as music, architecture, vestments, and other external aids may change with the times. But the liturgy, which derives its language ultimately from the Bible, must always remain faithful to the Word of God, no matter what changes may take place in the world around us.

The word liturgy is by no means one that can be taken for granted. It has all kinds of different meanings and connotations for people who use it. There are those within Christendom who look upon it with grave suspicion as the effort of a little group of specialists who seek to impose a bookish worship upon a Church accustomed to freedom. They are likely to say that they do not wish to be hampered by a book when all that is needed is the inspiration of the Holy Spirit. On the other hand, there are those who look to the movement of recovery of the liturgy as the single most important aspect of the reformation of the Twentieth Century. They see in the liturgy not only a bridge over which men may join ranks in the Body of Christ with Christians of every century, but also the means by which a divided Christendom may be healed of its many divisions. And in between these two are many thousands more of devout Christians who are not quite sure what it means, but who are eager to learn if someone will only take time to explain it to them.

Neither group can take the position of the other lightly. Indeed, the Reformed stance on the liturgy has been precisely

1

in the middle between the two: "... forms of prayer are given without any idea of restraining her members to any fixed standards of prayer," leaving to the "piety and gifts of her ministers to conduct the ordinary solemnities of the sanctuary in a manner most acceptable to God, and most edifying to His people."[1] For this reason, it is expected of her ministers that they will be informed by the liturgy, and be good students of Scripture, theology and the right conduct of public worship. If they depart from the liturgy, they should do so in the above spirit, and present the Word of God "decently and in order" in as good a fashion or better than is found in the liturgy.

Even in non-liturgical worship, so-called, there is more liturgical influence than some may have supposed. Take, for example, the Doxology and Gloria Patri. These are ancient liturgical pieces sung by almost every congregation every Lord's Day. They are fixed, they are sung, and they have Greek and Latin titles, respectively — the very things which advocates of free worship say they dread. Yet by their long and universal usage these have become almost second nature for evangelical Christians of almost every denomination. When one adds to these the Ten Commandments (which were sung by the congregation in Calvin's Geneva liturgy), the Psalms, hymns, creed, prayers and sacraments, we have what approaches a full course of liturgy. These are the components of worship in almost all congregations, whether they are called by the name liturgy or simply the "order of worship."

The surest way to prevent an abuse of the liturgy is for the congregation to insist upon its right to participate in it, to have the Word of God preached and *heard* (very important!) in its purity, and to have the sacraments performed according to the command of Christ. If these things are done as they should be, there is little doubt that the Church which gathers around them will be in truth the Church of Christ, and the worship which follows will be "in spirit and in truth."

The liturgy is never properly used when a minister reads or recites before a silent congregation. The liturgy is the work of the people — the corporate Body of Christ — clerical and lay, at worship. The language is sometimes spoken, sometimes sung;

[1]Preface to the 1793 edition of *Constitution of The Church in America.*

the form may be provided by prayer, Scripture, sacraments, creed or hymn; the action may be by minister and people, or by each in turn. Properly understood, the liturgy provides every man with his part in worship as the Spirit of God moves over His people and they make their responses.

HISTORICAL SKETCH OF THE PEOPLE OF GOD AT WORSHIP

The Christian Church has received its mode of worship from historical sources which are recorded in the Scriptures, and derived from the long story of the people of God. It has been the purpose of the committee which revised our liturgy to reflect faithfully the service as shaped over the centuries. Beginning with the service of the synagogue, continuing to the upper room where our Lord broke bread on the night in which He was betrayed, and following through centuries of formation, reformation and recovery, we seek to show the manner in which it is still fitting for the assembled congregation to express what they believe and intend to be in the world today.

The Synagogue Service

During the Exile, the Jewish people of necessity had to develop some kind of worship to replace the temple service. This was the beginning of the synagogue. At the heart of it was the study of the Torah, accompanied by the shema, blessings, prayers, and the peoples' amen.[2] The gradual development of a liturgy, probably reflecting temple worship, brought about a synagogue service something like the following:

> Prayer of Adoration
> The Shema (the Jewish Creed)
> Scripture Lessons
>   one from the Law
>   one from the Prophets
> Common Prayers
> The Peoples' Amen
> An Exposition or Sermon
> The Benediction

[2]Osterley & Robinson: A History of Israel, Vol. 2, pp. 137, 138 OXFORD UNIVERSITY PRESS; 1939.

Something of the above nature was quite likely the form of the worship of the synagogue by the First Century. When our Lord "came to Nazareth where He had been brought up, He went to the synagogue, as His custom was on the sabbath day" (Luke 4:16). The description of what followed, how He stood up to read, how they gave Him the book of the prophet Isaiah, and the exposition which followed, all are true to what we know from other sources to be the nature of the synagogue service. It was the reading of the Scriptures in a setting of prayer and praise. When we recall that a hymn was sung by Jesus and His disciples at the conclusion of their last supper together (Matthew 26:30), we have the components of worship in most Protestant churches since the Reformation.

The Upper Room

It was natural for the early Christians to begin with the Synagogue Service since it was their heritage. But, of course, they did not stop there. Having received from the Lord the command to continue the breaking of bread and the drinking of the cup until His coming (1 Corinthians 11:23-26), the Service of the Upper Room followed as the climax of the Synagogue Service. In due time the Synagogue Service would come to be known as the Service of the Word, and the communion was the response of the people to what they had heard. The two were combined in a single, full celebration of the whole course of the history of the chosen people, the first being all that is denoted by the phrase "the law and the prophets," while the second is the celebration of the coming of our Lord Jesus Christ, His incarnation, passion, resurrection and continuing presence in the Church through the Holy Spirit.

The Early Church

While the intent of the early church is perfectly clear — an effort to maintain the heritage of both Synagogue and Upper Room — succeeding generations have not been very successful in holding the two together. Intended to be two in one, as an elipse has its two focal points, the centuries have witnessed a constant tendency to rend them asunder. Such early writers as

Justin Martyr (155 A.D.) and Hippolytus (circ. 200 A.D.), who gave us an early liturgy in the *Apostolic Tradition*, show plainly how the first Christians worshipped. They linked together the Synagogue and the Upper Room, the Word and the Sacrament, in a single celebration of the history and redemption of the people of God.

The difficulty in holding them together probably arose at the point where a distinction was made between catechumens and the faithful. Those under instruction in the rudiments of the Christian faith, called catechumens, and even strangers, were permitted to attend the service through the sermon, but when the transition was made from Synagogue to Upper Room, from the Service of the Word to the Lord's Supper, all non-communicants were dismissed. Then followed the celebration of the Supper or the Eucharist.

It was during the Middle Ages that the Service of the Word gradually slipped from view, while more and more elaboration was added to the latter portion of the service, until the Mass emerged.

The Reformation

When the reformers came on the scene in the Sixteenth Century, they struck hard against the abbreviated form of worship found in the Mass. They all agreed upon the necessity of restoring the two-fold nature of Christian worship. They considered the sermon as essential to the nurture of Christian souls as they did the sacraments. But in their attempt to restore the Word of God with the sermon to its proper place, they came upon a stubborn fact which resulted in another error. It now became commonplace to conclude worship with the sermon, leaving out the celebration of the Eucharist except four times a year.

Calvin's experience with the Council in Geneva was typical. He wanted the Lord's Supper celebrated every Lord's Day, but knowing this to be unfeasible, he proposed a monthly observance. Even this was more than the Council would permit, so the custom of a quarterly communion was begun. With his keen appreciation of posterity, Calvin noted that, while accepting the necessity thrust upon him, he nevertheless trusted that future generations would correct this error. To this day, more than 400 years later, too many Reformed and Presbyterian churches let this exhortation go unheeded. The worship of our churches on an average Lord's Day is still only half a service, the sermon without the sacrament, based on the Synagogue Service. There is still some unfinished business in the Church for the present and future generations.

The Liturgical Revival

The present revival of Christian worship is moving decisively in the direction of the restored full service of Word and Sacrament. Those who have revised the liturgy of the Reformed Church have held this principle firmly before them. We are quite aware that it would be too much to hope for the restoration of the full service all at once. But there is a middle stance we can take which is both feasible and faithful to our heritage. The Service of the Lord's Day in the *Liturgy, 1968* recommends that the sermon be restored to its rightful place soon after the Scripture lessons are read. This, of course, takes place at the pulpit, the prominent symbol of the Service of the Word found in every Protestant Church. Now we seek to call attention to the other universal symbol of the Christian Church — the holy table — and restore it to its proper place as a focal point in worship.

Historically, the table appeared in the meeting houses of the Christians before the pulpit did. When they gathered for worship the table was set before them. The Service of the Word at first was the recitation of the memoirs of the Apostles, the full contents of one of the Gospels, probably spoken from memory by one of the presbyters or deacons, without the aid of pulpit or lectern. Only later was the addition of a full course of Scripture made, probably at the time when the canon was agreed upon. As a response to the Scripture service, including the sermon, the people brought their gifts to the table. The offering was of two kinds: alms for the poor, and gifts of bread and wine for the Lord's Supper. In a real sense there is an important link between the offering and the communion. Both

were received at the table and were a part of the response of
the people which led directly into the communion. This was
preceded, however, by the prayers of the congregation, first
among which is the great prayer of thanksgiving, or EUCHAR-
ISTIA, from which we receive the word Eucharist.

In the newly revised *Liturgy* of the Reformed Church, the
committee have placed an innocent-looking little rubric, or
direction, on page 14. Following the sermon and prayer for
blessing on the Word, these words appear:

> "The movement of the service now goes from the
> pulpit to the table, where the minister will receive
> the offerings of the people. . . ."

After the singing of the Doxology, the ushers return to their
places, and then,

> "While at the table, the minister shall lead in
> prayers of thanksgiving and intercession, conclud-
> ing with the Lord's prayer."

Moving the service to the communion table at this point does
two important things: (1) it calls attention to the second focal
point of worship, with the minister facing the congregation
from the table with the people gathered before him; and (2) it
calls attention to the nature of the offering. Whether our gifts
are bread and wine or cold, hard cash, we are bringing them to
the Lord in response to the preaching of His Word. We are
doing more than taking the collection. We are recalling in a
vivid way the saying of Jesus that when two or three are
gathered together in His name, He is there in the midst of them.
We respond to His presence by giving both our gifts and ourselves in His service.

This sequence of worship follows the same natural procedure
from pulpit to table on every Lord's Day whether or not the
sermon is accompanied by the sacrament. Congregations which
have followed this service have reported that once they became
accustomed to it, they found that having the prayers climax the
service made this part of worship much more meaningful to
them. Furthermore, by placing the sermon in closer proximity
to the Scripture, of which it is the exposition, the sermon gained

in meaning as well. Should the day ever come when we once again feel impelled to break bread at His table in the Lord's name as a regular part of the weekly service, we have the pattern for it ready to go. Not only would it unite us with the practice of the early church, but it would bring us into the common heritage of Christendom, including Orthodox and Roman Catholic as well as many families of Protestants.

The Liturgy and the Reformed Faith

Members of the Reformed Church are aware of the fact that the theology of the church stems in large measure from the Heidelberg Catechism. It has shaped the theology and nourished the faith of its members for more than 400 years. Written in 1563, there have been few documents which have approached the simplicity and grandeur of its essential truths, and the recent quadricentennial gave new impetus to its influence on both sides of the Atlantic.

While making much of the anniversary of the catechism, and rightly so, the Reformed Church was almost silent about another anniversary, which would surely have seemed strange to our forefathers, especially Ursinus, the chief author of the catechism. For almost simultaneously with the catechism in 1563 there also appeared another document of equal importance; the Liturgy of the Reformed Church in the Palatinate. It was not by accident that the two appeared together. The two documents were meant to be companion pieces, setting forth simultaneously the faith of the church and the expression of that faith in worship.

The probability is that, like the catechism, the liturgy had Ursinus for its chief author, although no one is mentioned by name. The preface was written by the Elector Frederick, who speaks of several authors but names none. While we admire the modesty of these self-effacing men, we would be grateful if their names had been left to us as well as the fruit of their labors.

Our major concern here however, is the all-important principle of the companionship of confession and liturgy. The catechism appeared as an integral part of the Church Ordinances, and was given a place between the form for baptism and the Lord's Supper. Faith and order, doctrine and worship, were held in unity; the catechism supplied the norm for the faith of the church. The liturgy supplied the form for the expression of that faith in worship.

While the catechism has retained its form for these four centuries, the liturgy has had quite another fate, at least as far as the Reformed Church in America is concerned. There is unquestionable evidence that it (the liturgy) immediately found its way into the Netherlands where, along with the catechism, it enjoyed widespread use.

In an edition of the liturgy translated by Petrus Dathenus in 1566, the German original was so slavishly followed that Dutch congregations in the "prayer after the sermon" were making intercession "especially . . . for the Gracious Elector, Duke Frederick, Count Palatine: also for the elector's gracious spouse; and for the young gentleman, his son." This lapse (for so it seems to have been), was corrected in the edition of 1568, when we find Dutch congregations making the petition: "Also we pray especially for the noble and wise Lords, the States General of the United Netherlands."

The content of that liturgy is interesting. It contained:

A form for infant baptism
A short examination into the faith of those who
    desire to join the Church
A form for the administration of the Lord's Supper
A form for the confirmation of marriage
Prayer before sermon on Sunday
Prayer before catechetical instruction
Prayer and confession of sin before sermon
    on weekdays
Prayer after sermon
Prayer before eating
Two prayers for the sick and the tempted
Prayer at the burial of the dead

It was not until the Synod of Dort in 1618-19, that a form of baptism for adults was added, and later an order of worship for the Lord's Day was included.

While the major outline of our liturgy is definitely traceable to the Palatinate, there were two other sources from which additional influence came. One was the liturgy composed by John A'Lasco, the pastor of a Walloon congregation which had found safety in London; and, of course, Calvin's liturgies of Geneva and Strasbourg, which were later to become the basis of the *Book of Common Prayer*. The principle remains the same, however: The confessional churches sought to express their faith in their mode of worship and set it forth in a liturgy. The Reformed Churches of Geneva, the Palatinate, the Netherlands, France, England and Scotland were identical in this respect. As early as 1574, the Provisional Synod of Dort (not to be confused with the National Synod to be convened 44 years later) had directed all ministers under its jurisdiction to use the same forms of public prayer.

Along with their liturgies, however, the Reformed Churches maintained a keen sense of liberty. Nowhere is this more clearly stated than in the preface to the 1793 edition of the *Constitution of The Church in America*. The following excerpt from that document voices this principle clearly.

"In consequence of that liberty wherewith Christ hath made His people free, it becomes their duty as well as their privilege, openly to confess and worship Him according to   the dictates of their consciences. . . . Her mode of worship is expressed in the liturgy where forms of several prayers are given without any idea, however, of restraining her members to any particular terms or fixed standards for prayer. Firmly believing that the gifts of the Holy Spirit for the edification of Zion in every age are promised and bestowed, the Reformed Dutch Church judges it sufficient to show in a few specimens the general tenor and manner in which public worship is performed, and leaves it to the piety and gifts of her ministers to conduct the ordinary solemnities of the sanctuary in a manner they judge most acceptable to God, and most edifying to His people."

While our liturgy went through numerous successive revisions during the intervening years, most of them very minor, nearly 50 years had passed since the last one, before the General Synod of 1950 appointed a committee to bring the church's worship abreast of the times. In the lengthy interval all kinds of strange things had happened: creed and commandments had almost disappeared from worship; the forms of prayer were largely disregarded and replaced by the "pastoral prayer" (often, with deadly accuracy, designated the "long prayer"); the lectionary was almost completely ignored. In short, the rich liturgical heritage of the Reformed Church was nearly lost (with the exception of the forms for baptism, the Lord's Supper, and the ordinations). The liberty granted to the churches had proved a mixed blessing.

The *Liturgy* of 1968 is an attempt to bring the Reformed Church to a new awareness of her heritage, both liturgically and theologically. To recover liturgy without theology would be to have form without substance. A church whose worship expresses a faith and a theology as the spirit of God moves through pulpit and pew to a lively participation in Word and Sacrament is a church that believes with its heart and expresses with its lips the living faith. The liturgy is not an end in itself: it is the servant first of the Scriptures, and then the medium of expression of the faith of the Church.

Before leaving the subject, special mention should be made of the Psalms, particularly in the Reformed Church with its great heritage of Psalm singing. No one who has heard the singing of the Psalms in Dutch — and many of them in English, as well — will soon forget their majestic melodies and the deep feeling with which they are sung. This, too, is part of our liturgical heritage, the work of the people. We will not dwell on the subject for it would soon take us into a consideration of *The Hymnbook*, and that is another question in itself. Suffice it to say that we are glad to see that so many of the Psalms have found their way back into *The Hymnbook*. No one would say that the singing of psalms or hymns is without spirit because they are in a book. It would be truer perhaps to say that they teach us to sing with spirit. "I will sing with the spirit and I will sing with the mind also," says the Apostle Paul. This is precisely what the liturgy is supposed to do. The whole liturgy is meant to be a teaching vessel that puts spirit into the worship of the people.   — Garrett C. Roorda

Chapter II

THE ORDER OF WORSHIP

The conduct of public worship is one of the most satisfying and challenging of all opportunities given to the minister of the Gospel. To do it well should be his constant objective, calling for the utilization of all his skills — careful thought, patient preparation and regular rehearsal. The minister is the key to worship that stimulates, lifts up and refreshes the people of God; but it is not a one man show. He is in a sense the producer, the director and a player in the drama; but the congregation should be made to feel that this is their service, too. The Amen from the people, the hymns, psalms, prayers, offering, indeed, every portion of the service, should be directed to the glory of God in such a way that the congregation may literally say with the Psalmist:

"I was glad when they said to me,
'Let us go to the house of the Lord!' " (Psalm 122:1)

This note of gladness should be evident in every word that is spoken, and it should be reflected in the face and manner of the minister as well as in the words of his mouth. A congregation will very quickly respond to inspired leadership in worship from the pulpit. It is equally true that they will respond to a lackluster performance in the pulpit with lethargy, and possibly even reward the minister by falling asleep during the sermon, if not sooner. If the expectations of the worshippers have been turned off by a lifeless conduct of the liturgy, they are not to be blamed if they drowse through a discourse that does not lift them. A minister who has given real attention to putting joy and gladness into the expressions of praise and prayer in the liturgy is likely to show the same qualities when it comes to preaching. Liturgy conducted with spirit can even redeem a mediocre sermon, but, of course, can never be a substitute for good preaching.

12

I. The Approach to God

The outline of the order of worship is given under three headings: The Approach to God, The Word of God and The Response to the Word. This chapter will seek to give an account of the meaning and content of each of the component parts of worship, including a rationale where needed.

In a way, the Approach is an attempt to find a liturgical answer to the question of Micah:

"Wherewith shall I come before the Lord,
And bow myself before the high God?" (Micah 6:6)

This question, together with its answer,

"He hath shown thee, O man, what is good;
And what doth the Lord thy God require of thee
But to do justly, to love mercy, and to walk
humbly with thy God?" (Micah 6:8)

should play a prominent part in all our worship. It points us beyond our liturgy, and beyond the four walls within which we worship to the continuation of the service of God in the world. Justice, mercy, and a humble walk with God must find their real expression in the home, in the marketplace and everywhere our workaday lives may take us. The liturgy seeks to begin the service, but its culmination must come in the establishment of a rhythm of worship and work as the people of God serve Him in the world. In a very real sense, the liturgy is a rehearsal for life. It is the celebration of every meaningful phase of life — birth, marriage, work, death — all permeated by the love of God in Christ. We make our approach to God in order to learn His ways so that we may serve Him in the world.

The Votum

"Our help is in the name of the Lord who made heaven and earth."

With this simple declarative sentence from Psalm 124:8, the liturgy of the Reformed Church makes its beginning. It is by no means the exclusive property of the Reformed Church, but it is, nonetheless, a distinguishing trade mark.

The committee pondered long and hard over the retention of this word, Votum. It is unfamiliar, it is not found in many dictionaries, and its form is Latin rather than English when we have been trying to simplify our language. Then why use it? Because no substitute could be found. It is not a prayer, it is not an invocation, nor is it simply a sentence from Scripture or a call to worship. It is a declaration of faith and theology. It is our own distinctive way of saying who we are and whom we serve. God the Lord made His name known to Moses at the burning bush: YHVH — I AM WHO I AM. We come to worship in His name. God the creator is everywhere present, but especially in the assembly of the congregation who worship in His name. He has been pleased to reveal Himself to us in these latter days through His Son Jesus Christ who has commissioned us to do His work in the world. The votum separates this gathering from all other groups in the world, and sets the tone for what is to follow. The courts, the congress, the school board and the directors of the bank have their own way of calling their meetings to order. So does the Church. Our business is the service and worship of God. We gather in the name of the Lord and in His presence. There is nothing magical or mystical about it. We do not have any secrets. But we do have a faith, and that we seek to declare.

This is important to us both theologically and liturgically. We have been given the promise that "where two or three are gathered together *in my name,* there am I in the midst of them." We are to take this promise as it is given, and believe it. This is one of the differences between the votum and an invocation. If we take Him at His word, it is unnecessary to beseech Him with prayers to be present when He has declared that He *is* present.

There is one more important aspect of this word, that brings us to the heart of the theology of Christian worship. Worship takes place in the presence of God, the real presence. We have no ark of the presence, no holy of holies, no secret shrine. We have only this simple declaration to the faithful — "In my name." He is really present. Although we usually associate these words with the Lord's Supper, they permeate the whole structure of the service throughout Word and Sacrament. To assume anything else would mark us as unbelieving ones who do not trust their Lord at His word. The votum sounds the note of faith in His real presence; anything else would be to assume His real absence. Many Protestants have shied away from the doctrine of the real presence because of its unfortunate past associations with theological controversy. We do not attempt to define the nature of His presence, and would not if we could. We are content in the knowledge that we have the assurance of His presence. This may come to us in the prayers, the hymns, the preaching and hearing of His word, or the breaking of bread at His table. Any or all of these may communicate the presence of God to His people.

When the minister of the word of God addresses the congregation with these words, fraught as they are with all the above implications, he should do so with conviction and authority, with solemnity and joy. His tone and manner should convey such confidence to the people that they will come to reverent attention, and give their hearts and minds to the drama of worship now about to unfold.

The votum may be spoken from the pulpit if this is the place where the minister would naturally stand to begin the service. Or, if the table is so located, he may stand at the table facing the congregation. Calvin did it this way at Geneva. But no matter what Calvin did, the important thing is that these words be spoken and heard in a way that says clearly: God is here. Let us worship and adore Him.

The words "In the name of the Father, and of the Son, and of the Holy Spirit," (Matthew 28:19) are also appropriate to use as the votum.

Sound the Amen

How reluctant are many Protestants to make use of the Amen in their worship! In the synagogue service it was an integral part of praise and the peculiar property of the people. It was to be said in response to the commandments (Deuteronomy 27:15). It was the response of the people to the song of thanksgiving that was sung when the ark of the covenant was brought into the tent (I Chronicles 16:36). At the time of the rebuilding of Jerusalem, and the reading of the law by Ezra, the priest, the people answered, "Amen, Amen." (Nehemiah 5:13; 8:6).

It was so much a part of worship among the early Christians that the Apostle Paul could write to the Corinthians, "If you bless with the spirit, how can anyone in the position of an outsider say the Amen to your thanksgiving when he does not know what you are saying?" (I Corinthians 14:6). It was assumed without question that even a newcomer in the congregation would expect to sound the Amen.

Note that it is not part of the prayer, and is not spoken by the one who says the prayer. It is the prerogative of the people to supply it. Ministers and others who lead in prayer publicly should lead the congregation to the conclusion of the prayer by saying, ". . . through Jesus Christ our Lord," or other familiar formula, and leave the response to the people. Even if they do not pick up the idea immediately, it is better to conclude the prayer without the Amen than it is for the minister to assume something that does not belong to him. Perhaps this will require some retraining of both ministers and congregations, but it will be well worth the effort if this ancient custom of the people at worship can be restored to them. As we sing in Joachim Neander's magnificent hymn of praise, Lobe den Herren: (*The Hymnbook*, No. 1)

> "Let the Amen
> Sound from His people again:
> Gladly for aye we adore Him."

For the most part, we sing the Amen lustily at the end of our hymns. Why not say it with equal vigor at the conclusion of our prayers?

The people's Amen should come at least in the following places: after the votum, at the conclusion of all prayers, after the salutation; after the commandments or summary of the law; after the creed; after the benediction, and at any other point in the service where the Spirit moves one to say it.

The Sentences

The votum is followed by one or more sentences from the Scriptures, varied according to the church year. Those given on pages 7 and 8 in the *Liturgy* are but the merest beginning of a wealth of such materials which may be found throughout the Scriptures. The Psalms especially abound in joyful expressions of praise and thanksgiving which set the tone of worship. While praise is the general note to be sounded, the penitential seasons of Advent and Lent should have their own special emphasis. A skillful selection of sentences can be one of the most edifying features of The Approach to God.

Salutation

The salutation is quite literally a greeting. It is spoken by the minister with his hand upraised. It is not a prayer. It is a point in the service where both minister and congregation should have their heads up and their eyes open, just as we would in exchanging any other greeting. Once again, the Amen of the people is the natural response. It is followed by the hymn of praise if there was no processional hymn, otherwise the congregation are seated following the salutation and the service moves to the prayer of confession.

The Prayer of Confession

If the praise we have sung has in any wise helped us, with Isaiah, to "see the Lord, high and lifted up;" if in any sense our hymn of praise has fulfilled the theme, "Holy, holy is the Lord of Hosts; the whole earth is full of His glory," we are now ready to humble ourselves before the divine majesty and confess our sin. Here, again, the confession may well be introduced in a direct conversational manner by the minister, using the sentence on page 8 or the simple invitation to join in the confession of sin. This prayer should be said in unison by all. The samples of prayers given on pages 8 to 10 are a good start, but this is also an opportunity for the minister and other members of the congregation to exercise their ministry in composing prayers most suited to the congregation's special needs. It is also wise to allow a minute of silence for private confession or meditation. This may be followed by the singing or saying of the Kyrie (Lord, have mercy upon us) by the congregation and choir. (*The Hymnbook*, Nos. 570, 571)

The Words of Assurance

The announcement of God's forgiveness and mercy should be spoken with a joyful conviction that God has visited and redeemed His people. It is good news and this should be evident both in the words themselves and the manner in which they are spoken.

The Law and Its Summary

The Heidelberg Catechism places the Ten Commandments under the subject of Thanksgiving or Gratitude. It is the belief of the committee that it is the most appropriate position also in the liturgy. The Law is not so much that which moves us to the confession of sin as it is the pointing to the way in which we should now walk. The liturgy of the Reformed Church is one of the few in Christendom which has retained the Ten Commandments. It is not necessary to read them in detail. It is perhaps sufficient to say, "You shall not covet," rather than go into the details of an agrarian life which may or may not apply in the Twentieth Century. The Law should not be concluded without its Summary, to love God and our neighbor, which is the Gospel emphasis.

Psalter and Gloria Patri

Following the announcement of forgiveness, the giving of The Law as the way in which to go, the praise of the Church now bursts forth. It is appropriate for the people to rise to praise God with a Psalm which may be any of the readings provided in the *Liturgy*, or, even more appropriately, the Canticles beginning on page 356, noting as suggested the tunes in *The Hymnbook* to which they may be sung. Numbers 586 through 596 in *The Hymnbook* are also a fitting part of praise at this point.

II. The Word of God

There should be a distinct sense of the completion of The Approach to God before the Service of the Word begins, following the singing of praise as in the Glori Patri or a canticle. The approach may have been conducted from the holy table. If so, the service should now move to the pulpit. The minister's entry into the pulpit carries with it the authority of the Word of God. He is the Minister of the Word.

The Prayer For Illumination

Specimen Prayers For Illumination may be found on pages 386 and 387. They should be brief and directed toward a right understanding of the Scriptures under the guidance of the Holy Spirit.

The Lessons

The less said the better in introducing the lessons. A simple statement of chapter and verse is sufficient. The lectionary, pp. 200-207, should be of much help to minister and congregation in selecting a varied course of readings according to the church year. While but one lesson is given, it is well for there to be two lections at each service, one from the Old Testament and one from the New. These should be added by the minister himself. Responses to the Scriptures may be found in *The Hymnbook*, Numbers 547-550.

Confession of Faith

The confession of faith and a hymn are placed in this position in the belief that some congregations will prefer to respond to the reading with the Apostles' or Nicene Creed. Other congregations may prefer to have the creed in the service at the table as part of their response to the Word. The real objective at this point is to let the congregation respond with their own confession of faith and the singing of a hymn as the service moves toward the sermon. At the conclusion of the hymn the minister should be in the pulpit ready to preach.

The minister may appropriately preface his sermon with the sentence, "Let the words of my mouth and the meditation of my heart be acceptable in thy sight, O Lord, my strength and my redeemer." The sermon may be concluded with an Ascription of Glory such as: "Now unto Him that is able to prevent you from falling, and to present you faultless before the only wise

God our Savior, be honor and glory, dominion and power, both now and forever, world without end. Amen."

Prayer For Blessing on the Word

An Ascription of Glory as above is entirely sufficient at the conclusion of the sermon. For those who wish to add or sub-stitute a Prayer For Blessing on the Word, let it be brief and to the point. Prayers such as "For grace to use the Word aright," as on page 418 in the *Liturgy* are an example. In any case, it should not be either a summary or a re-hash of the points already made in the sermon. *Keep it short.*

III. The Response to the Word

When the service moves to the table the congregation have left the Synagogue and are entering the Upper Room. What takes place here is, above all, a service of prayer. It may begin with a little processional in much the same manner as at the beginning of the service. If communion is to be celebrated the gifts of the people may be brought to the table by the ushers, immediately followed by others appointed to bring in the gifts of bread and wine. Whether they are placed on the table or set aside is of little importance. The prayers of thanksgiving and intercession now follow. If communion is also to be celebrated, the service continues as on page 65 in the *Liturgy*. If communion is not celebrated, the service proceeds to the general prayers as on pages 387-400. These are good examples of general prayers to which may be added special intercessions according to the need of the congregation. The prayers should be brief and varied so that the congregation can follow them clearly and respond to each with the Amen.

The Offering and Doxology

As the offerings of the people are brought to the table the congregation may stand and sing the Doxology. The ushers may very well stand with the minister while the prayer of dedication is said. This is also a good place for a layman to exercise his ministry. In some churches a layman announces the offering,

receives the gifts at the table, and says the prayer of blessing. This is one more way in which laymen may participate in the service and give added emphasis to the response of the people. Following the prayer of dedication the ushers may retire and the congregation be seated.

General Prayers

The general prayers should be said from the table in exactly the same position as during the communion. Thus, if the service culminates either with the Lord's Supper or with the prayers, the sequence is the same and the focus of the service taking place around the table is the climax. The general prayers should conclude with the entire congregation joining in the prayer our Lord taught His disciples. This is followed by the closing hymn.

The Benediction

The benediction is said while the minister is still at the table, completing the circle of those gathered around it, and not, say, from the back of the church. It is spoken with both hands upraised, head up and eyes open. It is not a prayer. It is the farewell, just as the salutation was the greeting. The people should reply with the Amen, and very shortly thereafter be on their way rejoicing.

— Garrett C. Roorda

Chapter III

THE ORDERS FOR THE SACRAMENT OF BAPTISM

No rite in the Church is as ancient in authority and practice as the sacrament of baptism. The New Testament has more to say about baptism than about the Lord's Supper. In the early Church the sacrament of baptism was its prime mystery, and the eucharist had its significance within baptismal incorporation into Christ.

Only adult baptisms are specifically recorded in the New Testament, though it is not unreasonable to assume that infants may have been included whenever an entire family was baptized. We read of several households who received the sacrament, but only two individuals, the Ethiopian eunuch and the Apostle Paul were singularly baptized. Our Reformed orders for the administration of the sacrament also assume the corporate family nature of the sacrament in the sections on the meaning of baptism which include the phrase, "we and our children." The rite has significance for the entire household.

In recent years the validity of infant baptism has been seriously questioned, but no official change has been made in either doctrine or practice. A minister in the Reformed Church in America is bound to carry out his ministry of Word and Sacrament in harmony with the doctrine and order of his Church (Belgic Confession, Art. 34; Heidelberg Catechism, Questions 69-74), and it is the duty of classis to oversee that the ministers perform the rites of the Church in harmony with its standards of faith and practice. The forms for the administration of baptism are obligatory.

The Liturgy offers four orders for the administration of baptism. The first order (p.p. 26-33) is new and is designed only for the administration of *infant* baptism. The structure also differs from the long and abridged forms in the Liturgy of 1906. Instead of setting forth the meaning of baptism at the very

beginning, this form opens with a brief statement on the institution of baptism as commanded by our Lord in Matthew 28:18-20. This supports the Reformed doctrine that the validity of a sacrament depends upon whether our Lord commanded it. The new form makes it clear that baptism as well as the communion service is based upon divine institution.

The scriptural passages, of which one or more must be read, emphasize the covenantal character and unity of the sacrament.

The section on the meaning of the sacrament is a thorough revision of the old form. It does, however, retain the doctrinal order of the main divisions of the Heidelberg Catechism, (1) Our Sins and Misery, (2) Our Deliverance, and (3) Our Debt of Gratitude to God for Our Redemption.

The unpopular phrase that our children are "conceived and born in sin" has been omitted, but the doctrine of original sin is clearly maintained in the opening paragraph, "that we with our children are sinful by nature and under the judgment of God." Though greatly shortened, this section also retains the trinitarian nature of the sacramental activity by which the baptized infant is ingrafted into the body of Christ and securely maintained in it unto the resurrection to eternal life. The ethical obligation of the baptized is clearly stated in the third paragraph of this section, and emphasizes that the sacrament calls us "to new obedience." The guarantee that baptism is an effective sacrament lies in the fact that God has appointed it as the sign and seal of his eternal covenant of grace with us. As such it can never be an empty sign. The Belgic Confession beautifully states this in Article 33 on the sacraments, "The signs therefore are not vain or empty so as to deceive us: for Jesus Christ is their reality, without whom they would have no significance."

The baptismal prayer contains only three brief paragraphs but is both beautifully written and effectively pertinent. The first paragraph offers God thanks for his salvation of which baptism is its sign and seal. The second is a request that the sacrament may indeed be rightly used and that the candidate for baptism may become and remain a true member of Christ's Church.

This second part of the prayer implicitly confirms the reformed doctrine that a sacrament does not work automatically, but only as an instrument of the Holy Spirit upon whose power the entire

Church is dependent. John Calvin rightly observed that the Scriptures always refer to the Holy Spirit whenever questioned how we can be united to Christ. There is no inherent power in the sacrament outside of the Spirit of Christ. Therefore the Church calls upon God to sanctify the sacrament with his Word and Spirit lest the whole transaction be in vain. The connection of the sign and the reality signified is grounded solely in the Holy Spirit.

The third paragraph reminds us of the answer to the first question in the Heidelberg Catechism. The baptized infant is not his own but belongs to his faithful Saviour. In view of this, the Church renews her self-offering to him who has promised "to be our God and the God of our children."

The new form also incorporates the Confession of Faith in the words of the Apostles' Creed. This emphasizes the unity and catholicity of the Church and our Christian faith. The congregation unites in a reaffirmation of those things most surely believed among us.

The vows that are taken by the parents follow naturally upon the confession of faith, and assume some previous instruction in the nature of the obligations which are voluntarily accepted by them. *They* desire the sacrament for their child, and they should therefore clearly understand the nature of their obligations. Are the parents truly aware of the meaning of each question?

In the vows the parents declare their acceptance of the Gospel as revealed in the Holy Scriptures and confessed in the Apostles' Creed. They acknowledge that their child is "sinful by nature," which means that it falls heir to the condition of the human race. The vows emphasize the corporate nature of sin which no child can escape except through the grace of God as signified in the sacrament.

Parents pledge to educate the child in the faith into which it is baptized both by "precept and example." In some circles this vow has been interpreted to mean education in a private Christian school. Whatever value such training may have, it is doubtful that the vow can be so interpreted. To teach the "truth of God's Word" and "the way of salvation through Jesus Christ" is a personal obligation on the part of the parents and should not be handed over to other agencies, even though their assistance may be enlisted.

Another new feature which makes this first form so attractive is the involvement of the congregation in the covenant renewal of their vows. In this sacrament the entire congregation is confronted with their continual obligation "to sustain the fellowship of faith and life within the Church of Christ" for their children. This form sets the sacrament in the midst of the Church where it rightly belongs, for it is the Church which baptizes through its office of the ministry. To do this in private is to rob the congregation of its rights, joy and obligation.

After the baptism in the name of the triune God there follows a declaration, which, though not obligatory, completes the action with a statement of fact. Something did happen and that fact ought to be declared. Both the Belgic Confession and the Heidelberg Catechism state clearly that we are by baptism received and incorporated into the body of Christ, and these facts are made known in the public declaration. The baptized child is now counted among the covenant people of God and lives in the very sphere where God's grace is made known.

The prayer which closes the baptismal service beautifully summarizes all that is hoped for in this solemn rite. It opens with a joyful note of thanksgiving that our children have the privilege of being brought to the Lord. Then follows a fervent intercession for the continued blessing and guidance of the Spirit for the baptized, the parents and the entire Church.

The Alternate Forms

The second and third orders are considered alternate forms and may be used whenever desired. They are the familiar unabridged and abridged forms of the Sacrament of Baptism as found in the *Liturgy and Psalms*, issued in 1906, and are greatly beloved through long and honored usage in the Church. The unabridged form is a translation from the Dutch, but Charles W. Baird says that this form and the communion rite have a much longer history.

> Composed originally by Calvin in French, translated by Polhemus into the English, rearranged by A'Lasco

in Latin, then translated by Utenhoven into the Dutch, and abridged by Micronius, it was finally reviewed by Dathenus, and adopted in 1566 as the standard of worship in the Reformed Church of Holland.[1]

After several other minor revisions one Liturgy was adopted for the entire Church at the great National Synod of Dort (1618-19). This Liturgy contained one form for the administration of baptism.

When the American Church finally became independent from the Mother Church in Holland, it adopted the Dutch Liturgy with minor changes for its own use in this country, including our present unabridged form for the administration of baptism. Charles W. Baird claims that the Dutch formularies were translated into English by the Reverend Dr. Henry Livingston.[2]

Although this form has long and honored usage in our Church, many have found it too long and its language archaic. Not until 1906, however, was an alternate form provided in what is now known as the "abridged" form.

One immediately notes the lack of an appropriate introduction in the unabridged form. Liturgy is an action in which pastor and congregation participate. A particular rite which the people are about to perform should be properly introduced. It is confusing to begin reading the meaning of the sacrament without first calling the attention of the congregation to what they are about to celebrate.

The words of institution are also missing in this form, but it maintains the doctrinal structure of the three major divisions in the Heidelberg Catechism.

Some people object to the phrase, "that we with our children, are conceived and born in sin." They interpret this to mean that conception is sinful and birth a curse. Nothing could be further from the truth. The phrase simply means that from the time of conception and birth, every child participates in the sins of the human race. To be human means to be born in a world of sin and misery, a heritage which no one can escape.

---

[1]Charles W. Baird, *Presbyterian Liturgies*, p. 214.
[2]Op. Cit. p. 216.

We acknowledge this fact when we bring our children to be baptized.

Whenever infants are baptized according to this rite, Section I must be read. This paragraph is a defense of infant baptism. The supporting biblical references are convincing, but when baptism is claimed to have "come in the place of circumcision," it is based upon questionable exegesis, and therefore should not be in the liturgy. To compare baptism to the Old Testament rite is legitimate and has scriptural warrant. In the New Testament baptism is also compared to the flood and the Church to Noah's ark, but no one would say that baptism has taken the place of the flood or that the Church has taken the place of Noah's ark.

The introduction to the interrogation of the parents has a sentence which might well have been included in the first form. It has reference to the right use of the sacrament and warns against using it "out of custom and superstition." Too many parents still desire the sacrament for the wrong reasons.

The greatest difference in the interrogation of this form lies in the fact that it is not directly addressed to the parents. In the first form the parents are specifically addressed as "the parents of this child," but in the unabridged form the plural pronoun is used, "us and our children." This is a serious omission, for parents should be the primary if not the exclusive sponsors of the baptism of their children.

The first question in the interrogation specifically says that if we acknowledge the conditions stated, then our children "ought to be baptized." This would seem to imply the necessity for some kind of disciplinary action against members of the Church who neglect to have their children baptized. We must not deny our children the sign and seal of God's gracious covenant to which He entitles them.

The second question requires that parents believe in the teaching of the Old and New Testaments, and "in the Articles of the Christian Faith." The latter are generally believed to be the Apostle's Creed. In earlier times it was not unusual to recite the Creed at this time. As previously noted, the new baptismal form included the recitation of the Creed.

The third question is lamentably weak in that it only asks

parents to see "these Children" instructed in the Christian faith when they reach the years of discretion. This is vague and raises the question what parents must do before their children reach the age of discretion. Are they not responsible for their instruction at every age? The abridged form of 1906 happily omitted any reference to "years of discretion."

The unabridged and abridged forms have neither the congregational vows nor the declaration of the new status attained by the baptized child. This does not imply that the congregation has no responsibility or that the baptism according to this rite does not confer the same status. It merely means that the congregation is not reminded of these important facts whenever use is made of these forms.

Both forms provide a service for adult baptism, and though seldom used in the past, with the secularization of society and the missionary position of the Church in the world, we shall no doubt see an increase in the number of adult baptisms.

The adult forms stem from a combination of Dutch rites which were unified at the National Synod of Dort in 1619. The abridged form is both shortened and revised, though it retains the essential elements contained in the longer form.

Order for Adult Baptism and Admission to the Lord's Table

On page 47 the Liturgy provides a new order for adult baptism and admission to the Lord's Table. The institution, meaning of the sacrament and the prayer are the same as in the first order. This would indicate that baptism is one sacrament whether administered to infants or adults.

Adult baptism is also recognized as the public confession of faith, and the candidate's admission into membership in the Church.

Young people who are already baptized may also make a public confession of their faith through this form, but they are not re-baptized. They simply confirm before God and his Church the same faith into which they were baptized as infants and in which faith parents and congregation took responsibility to train and nurture them.

The adult vows have a strong confessional emphasis. The candidate acknowledges the faith of the Church in the Apostles'

Creed and the fact that he now knows himself to be delivered from all his sins. He pledges "to make faithful use of the means of grace," and to live in harmony with the teachings and the membership of the congregation. He freely offers his service, prayers and gifts to the Church as long as he lives. The congregation also pledge their confidence and affection to the new member. This is good and desirable, for it reminds everyone of his mutual responsibility to his Christian brothers and sisters.

The declaration of the new status is the same as in infant baptism with the exception that the adult is also said to be admitted to the Lord's table.

Baptism and Pastoral Care

Baptism is an event which requires the pastoral ministry of the Church. The blessings and obligations of this sacrament must not be obscured by ignorance. The joy and comfort of this holy rite must be felt by all who are involved in it. To that end it is necessary to give attention to a better and more systematic method of baptismal instruction. In too many congregations baptism is not much more than an archaic appendix with little or no meaning.

Regular pastoral instruction requires a fundamental understanding of the purpose and meaning of baptism. The instructor should be able to give the members of his congregation the main emphases of the sacrament. Briefly they are as follows: a) The sacrament emphasizes that God in His loving grace takes the initiative to redeem us. Before we are capable of doing any good, God already pledges His grace to us. The sacrament, therefore, is not a seal upon our piety or good works but upon the everlasting mercy of our covenant God. b) God is our Lord and Master. We are citizens of His kingdom and are subject to His authority. c) Baptism is also a visible sign of the comfort we have from God in every time of need. The fact that we are baptized signifies God's gracious pledge to see us through every difficulty. Whenever Martin Luther began to doubt, he was comforted by the fact that he was baptized a Christian. d) The congregation must also be taught that baptism involves the subject into a new family relationship. By faith every baptized person learns to live for his fellow Christians. He is obliged to be a help to his neighbor. e) Greater importance must be attached to the pastoral care of the baptized, both by the home and the Church. Each in his own way is responsible for the religious training of the children. Such training must be provided in every possible way. If traditional methods are inadequate, new ways must be found. The ultimate goal of family and Church is to bring the baptized infants to a public confession of Jesus Christ and admission to the holy table.

The Administration of Baptism

Three distinct steps are involved in the actual event of baptism. 1. The request by the parents. 2. The house visitation by the pastor. 3. The service in the church.

To whom should the request for baptism be made? Practice varies within the Church. In some places the request is made of the pastor while in other congregations, parents must come before the Board of Elders. The latter seems a good practice, because the elders are then better able to share in the pastoral responsibility which belongs to them.

The parents should know when and where they may come to request baptism for their children. The request affords another opportunity to remind parents of their obligations with respect to their children. These obligations represent a total commitment for the entire family.

The pastor or clerk should secure the Christian name, date and place of birth of the child to be baptized, and the full names of the parents. All baptisms should be properly recorded in a register kept for that purpose.

Though some people may not consider it necessary to have another meeting with the parents, it would seem desirable to make a more personal pastoral call at the home. Home life in the twentieth century may not be what it used to be, yet the family is still the basic unit through which it pleases God to channel His grace. In the privacy and intimacy of the home the significance of the sacrament as it affects the family may be discussed in greater detail. Opportunity for questions from the family is also an important aspect of this visit.

Furthermore, the pastor is able to discover something of the spiritual tone of the family. Are they devoted and dedicated Christians? Do they desire the sacrament out of custom or superstition? Are they ready to assume their family obligations under the covenant of grace? Is every aspect of the nature and administration of the sacrament clear to them?

Here the question may be raised whether at least one parent ought to be a communicant member of the local church in which the child is to be baptized. An amendment to the Constitution requiring such a regulation was defeated last year by a majority of the classes. Though opinions on this subject no doubt vary, primary consideration should be given to the child and the nature of the sacrament itself. Baptism must not become a legal rod to compel parents to become communicant members in order to have their children baptized.

A pastoral ministry, however, ought to seek diligently to win the parents to publicly acknowledge their faith and unite with the congregation in which their children are baptized.

Instead of raising legal barriers, it is so much better to confront parents with the grace of the gospel as signified in the sacrament. One should ask whether the parents believe that Jesus Christ is their Saviour and the Saviour of their children. Do they truly believe that their family belongs to this Saviour? These are better questions than the formal one, "Are you a member in good and regular standing in our church?"

Every mechanical detail should also be covered with the family. Where should the family sit? When do they come forward to make the vows and present the child? Should the parents alone be involved, or should other members of the family also gather around the baptismal font? Who should hold the child? And is it desirable to have the pastor take the child from the parents for the baptism? Or does he baptize it in the arms of either mother or father? Though custom varies, these details should be understood by everyone, lest the ceremony is marked by evident confusion. The pastor should be in full control of every detail in the service. Parents should be well informed of the procedure, and if possible, have in advance a copy of the order which will be used.

Since baptism is a Church sacrament, its administration should normally take place in a regular service of worship. The family of God joins in the celebration that a new member is born into their fellowship. An outline for the order of worship when baptism is celebrated is provided on page 6 in the Liturgy. In this form baptism follows the service of the Word and is considered to be the visible seal upon it. There are those who prefer the baptism at the beginning of the service as the symbol of entrance into the Church. Karl Barth says, "The order of worship should be as follows: at the beginning of the service, public baptism; at the end the Lord's Supper; between the two sacraments, the sermon, which in this way would be given its full significance."[3] If this order were followed we would indeed have a *recte administrare sacramentum et pure docere evangelium.*"[4]

When infants are to be baptized it is good practice to announce the names of the parents and their children before reading the form. If the candidate for baptism is an adult, only his name needs to be announced. This gives the congregation an opportunity to know who is being incorporated into the Church.

Should the form be read from the pulpit or in the chancel near the baptismal font? Since the didactic sections of the rite form a kind of service of the Word, it would seem appropriate to read this section from the pulpit. However, there is no good reason why it may not be read from the chancel.

After the prayer, the parents should be invited to come to the font with their children. It may be desirable to invite the entire family of the candidate to stand in the chancel with the parents. This emphasizes the covenantal and household character of the event and is an opportunity for a renewal of baptismal vows by and for the entire family. If the church does not have a stationary font in the chancel, an elder may assist by holding the baptismal bowl for the minister.

The congregation should stand for the Creed and the vows, but may be seated during the act of baptism. This generally gives a better opportunity for everyone to see the performance of the rite.

[3]Karl Barth, The Preaching of the Gospel, p. 25.
[4]Op. Cit., p. 25.

The child may be baptized in the arms of one of the parents, or the minister may take the child into his left arm and apply the water with the right hand. He may either dip his hand in the water and sprinkle it on the child, or cup his hand and pour it over the child. The official trinitarian formula is always used, beginning with the Christian names which the child is to bear, but he will not speak the family name. Only the Christian names will be written on the certificate of baptism, but in order to identify the child, the full names of the parents will also be given.

If the candidate is an adult, the minister should ask him to kneel for the act of baptism. Should an adult request immersion as a more desirable mode, arrangements might be made with a local Baptist congregation. If no such facilities are available, weather and other conditions permitting, arrangements might be made to baptize in a nearby body of water. Suitable garments may also be secured from a Baptist congregation.

The act of baptism by immersion requires a water depth well up to, or slightly above the waist. The minister places his left hand firmly around the back of the candidate's neck, gently places his right hand over the candidate's mouth, while the candidate holds both hands firmly on the minister's right arm. When the trinitarian formula is spoken, the minister will gently push the candidate backward under the water bending at the knees and keeping feet firmly on the bottom of the pool or stream. The buoyancy of the water will quickly help the candidate back upon his feet. An appropriate dressing room should be provided.

Baptism like birth can only take place once. The mode of baptism used does not affect its efficacy and a minister should therefore not knowingly baptize anyone who has already received the sacrament. Our Church has always recognized the validity of baptism regardless of where and by whom or by what mode the rite has been performed.

What about sponsors? In the Reformed Church the congregation is the sponsor, and therefore shares in the responsibility to the baptized children. Only the parents or guardians and the congregation should therefore be allowed to assume the vows.

What about an "emergency" baptism? Should this sacrament

be administered to the dying? Certainly the sacrament is not the substance of grace itself, and grace may be received from God without it. It is, however, the "sign and seal" of God's grace, and may therefore be of comfort and support to those who receive it and to their families. The government of the Reformed Church in America requires that 'The consistory shall make provision for the private administration of the sacraments in instances of sickness or other emergency. At least one elder shall be present with the minister on such occasions.'

Chapter IV

THE ORDER FOR THE SACRAMENT OF THE LORD'S SUPPER

(p. 63)

A.

Before giving attention to the content of this liturgy, a word may be helpful as to its order. From a study of the four accounts of the Last Supper in the New Testament (Matthew, Mark, Luke, and I Corinthians), it is evident that great care has been taken by the four authors to record the order of events in the Upper Room on the night in which our Lord was betrayed. To be sure, there was on that occasion an actual supper which no longer forms part of our celebration. But after due account has been taken of that fact, an order of events becomes very clear.

    a) He took
    b) He blessed
    c) He brake
    d) He gave

In our new liturgy we feel that it is important to maintain this New Testament order. After the first part of the service, therefore, it moves as follows:

    a) The minister and elders gather around the Table and it is uncovered. This represents "He took".
    b) There is a prayer of thanksgiving and blessing. This represents "He blessed".
    c) This is followed by the recitation of the words of institution, accompanied by the breaking of the bread and the lifting of the cup. This represents "He brake".
    d) The elements are then given to the elders and the people after the words of distribution. This represents "He gave".

A brief look at the order of events in the new liturgy will indicate that it seeks to make the order of our celebration conform to this early defined Scriptural outline. As we gather to "do this in remembrance of Him", we follow His example not only in word but in action.

B.

Any revision of any liturgy that seeks to do more than make minor amendments must be done in accordance with certain principles. The new Order for the Sacrament of the Lord's Supper is in many ways a radical departure from our previous forms. It will be helpful, then, at the outset to state the principles which have guided the creation of this new form.

a) Faithfulness to the New Testament understanding of the meaning of the Supper;

b) Responsiveness to the Reformed doctrine of the Supper as set forth in both the Belgic Confession and the Heidelberg Catechism;

c) Sensitivity to liturgical language which will be meaningful to Christians of the mid-twentieth century while still conveying the essentials of our historic faith.

When changes have been made from previous liturgical forms, these are the principals which have guided the changes. We shall have occasion to make allusion to them as we proceed with our discussion, but we wish them clearly stated at the beginning as the guidelines for revision.

Let us now examine the three principal parts of the service:

1. The words of instruction
2. The prayer of thanksgiving - blessing
3. The prayers of intercession

1. Nothing is more difficult than the revision of a form which has acquired rich emotional association through long centuries of use. That section of our traditional liturgy entitled "Meaning of the Sacrament" (p. 78) is certainly a primary example of this fact. An abridged form of it (p. 88) was adopted in 1906 but it was strictly an abridgement with no changes in either

language or content. No one can deny that it has provided spiritual nourishment for many generations of Reformed Christians. But tradition alone is no guarantee of the significance of any Reformed liturgy forever and even our most precious inheritances must be re-examined in the light of our three guiding principles.

Perhaps there is a prior question to be faced here and that is the continued usage of a didactic section in a liturgical form. In our new liturgy we have retained it because we believe that a statement of the faith of the Reformed Church in America about the meaning of this Sacrament is important at this point. As the rubric (p. 63) indicates, however, it is better if that part of the form which encourages self-examination can be read at a service of preparation.

Both of the alternatives offered are considerably shorter than our older forms were. The Supper is not the place for an exposition of the whole Christian faith but rather the place for a succinct statement of what the Reformed Church believes about the Supper. We can assume that because of our Reformed catechetical training, those who come to the Lord's Supper will be well-grounded in Christian doctrine. At this time and place the didactic ought not to dominate the devotional.

The older forms stress the faith that the Supper is the remembrance of the atoning death of Jesus Christ. The new order repeats that emphasis in both of its alternates by retaining much of the traditional language from the older forms. It clearly states our faith in the sacrificial death of our Lord and its remembrance as the occasion which calls us together at His Table.

A study of the relevant confessional passages (of Belgic Confession XXXV and Heidelberg Catechism, Questions 75-80), as well as John Calvin's discussion of the subject, will show that our older terms, designed as they were to confront the Roman Catholic teaching about the sacrifice of the Mass, do not really deal adequately with the Reformed doctrine of the real presence. Yet this is the heart of Calvin's teaching about the Supper. The new liturgy therefore has added a paragraph in language which is both Scriptural and Calvinistic to make our liturgical witness more consistent with our confessional posture.

We have further found that all contemporary study of the New Testament has emphasized the eschatological character of the Supper. From St. Paul's "Till he come" to Revelation's "I will come in and sup with him", the sacrament is seen as pledge and foretaste of the heavenly banquet which will mark the final victory of the Kingdom. As a church obedient to the Word, we have sought to make this witness evident in our understanding of the Supper. Accordingly, another paragraph has been added to express this important idea.

The older forms concluded with a strong assertion that the Supper is the basis for unity among brethren. This is a Scriptural note which should certainly be sounded, and is sounded very completely in the old unabridged form which bears a striking resemblance at this point to the *Didache*, the oldest surviving Christian liturgy (c. 125 A.D.).

2. We have recognized that prayer is an essential part of the Supper. Remembering that before He broke the bread in the Upper Room our Lord "blessed" it, we have sought to give the prayer this character. It is universally admitted that in Biblical language to "bless" is to "give thanks". Thanksgiving, therefore, should be the chief note of the prayer at the Table.

At this point the prayer in the unabridged form (p. 80) seems to be badly deficient. It contains no note of Thanksgiving which we believe is the basic requirement set forth by Scripture. The prayer in the abridged form (p. 85) certainly sought to remedy this lack. But in the position in which it is placed in that form, it violates the Scriptural order of Upper Room events. Furthermore, its language is that of the 19th Century and lacks the simplicity for which the new liturgy is striving.

In view of our peculiar Reformed emphasis, however, we have felt that one other subject should be included in this prayer at the Table. A study of Calvin or of the Reformed tradition makes it clear that it is only through the power of the Holy Spirit that Christ is present in His Supper. We must pray, therefore, for the presence of the Spirit without which the Supper will be only a naked and bare sign. We have sought to give expression to this historic Reformed witness in the way in which we have worded the prayer of thanksgiving and blessing, especially the part which follows the singing of the hymn, "Holy,

Holy, Holy". One of the great virtues of our original Table prayer (p. 80) was the way in which, almost alone among eucharistic prayers from the Reformation, it expressed the eschatological note of hope and expectation. Unfortunately, the substitute prayer of 1906 (p. 89) eliminated this aspect entirely. In the eucharistic prayer of the new liturgy (p. 66-67) a serious attempt has been made to restore this authentic emphasis of our Dutch Reformed heritage but in different language. Believing that this is also the Biblical emphasis, we have sought to make this prayer expressive of present joy as well as of future hope.

3. The intercessions with which the new liturgy closes are only suggestions, not mandatory forms. But their place at the end of the service may seem unusual. In other services, including that one currently in use, they occur much earlier in the service. Why have they been placed at the very end, after the Thanksgiving psalm? The answer is that by placing them here we have sought to emphasize the often neglected truth that the Supper is not a shrine but an instrument by which God's people are strengthened for their work and witness in the world. The assurance which the Supper gives us is never selfish assurance but always assurance for effective witness, just as election to the people of God is not for enjoyment but for responsibility. As God's people we are both summoned and sent.

Having received the holy bread and wine, therefore, before we leave the Table, we are reminded of those who stand in need of our witness. Having begun our witness to them by lifting them up before the throne of grace, we go out into the world to continue our witness as a priestly people. This is the reason why the committee has placed the intercessions at the end of the Table Service.

C.

These notes have been very briefly presented in the hope that they may lead to serious theological study on the part of our Church. A liturgy is something which ought not to be changed lightly. But neither ought it to be retained out of custom, superstition, or even idolatry. The committee therefore urged the Church to study this proposed liturgy for the Supper in the light of the Word of God and our historic confession, as well as the needs of contemporary man.

Some Practical Suggestions for the Use of this Order

After the offering has been received and dedicated, the minister will return to the pulpit (or lectern) to read the "Meaning of the Sacrament" in one of the two alternate forms offered. Upon completing this reading, the minister customarily gives an invitation to the Table, since by long tradition the Reformed Church has not limited sharing in the bread and wine to her own members. No particular form or words is given but the invitation should be given in such a way that it is neither too strict or too relaxed. Historically the Reformed Church has always held that sharing in the Sacrament is the privilege of those who are communicant members of the Church. Hence an invitation to "all who love the Lord Jesus Christ" should be rejected as extending the invitation further than our tradition allows. On the other hand an invitation to "members of other Reformed congregations" is equally undesirable because it is too restrictive.

The following is offered as a suggestion. "To this Table we welcome in the Name of the Lord Jesus Christ all those who are members of his Church in any of its branches." Suitable words of Scripture such as Matthew 11:28, John 3:16, John 6:35, or Revelation 3:20 may be added.

During the singing of the hymn which follows the Instruction and the Invitation the minister shall take his place behind the Lord's Table facing the people. If the members of the Consistory are not already in their places, they should come forward at this time. In those congregations where the elements have been covered, they should be uncovered during the singing of this hymn.

There is a growing revival of the ancient custom of having members of Consistory or lay people bring the elements into the church and place them on the Table during the service. If this custom is to be used, it is at this time that such a bringing in of the elements should take place. It is a meaningful symbol of the fact that the bread and the wine are also our offering to God.

For the Great Prayer of Thanksgiving which follows the singing of the hymn, it is most appropriate that the congregation should remain standing through the singing or saying of the ancient hymn, "Holy, Holy, Holy". In a sense, these words represent more than a prayer; they are a great shout of acclamation, almost a hymn in themselves. After the triumphal termination of the thanksgiving, the congregation may be seated and bowed for a few moments of silence before the minister offers the prayer beginning, "Holy and righteous Father". The prayer is followed by what are traditionally known as the *manual acts*, that solemn moment in which we re-enact what our Lord did in The Upper Room on the night in which He was betrayed.

On the tray nearest to the minister there should be a piece of bread large enough to be clearly visible when he takes it and breaks it in view of the congregation as he repeats the words of our Lord. In those churches which have a chalice remaining from the days of the common cup, it will be helpful to place it on the Table for the minister to take in his hand as he repeats the words concerning the cup. If the chalice be used in this way, it is suggested that a little of the grape juice or wine be placed in it so that it is an actual symbol. If a chalice is not available, it is better for the minister to lift an entire tray of individual cups rather than a single one which is hardly a visible symbol.

In the most ancient practice of the Reformed Church it is the deacons who serve the elements to the congregation. Such is a fitting practice in view of Acts VI. Many congregations limit this service today to the elders, following the Presbyterian custom. There is no one way which is correct. Any church should be free to follow its own custom here.

The same rule applies to the order in which the Sacrament is given. The Reformed Church leaves it entirely up to local custom whether, for example, the minister shall receive the elements before or after the members of Consistory or the Congregation. In a number of congregations the custom has developed by which all present retain the elements until everyone has been served and so partake together. Other congregations prefer that each member should partake of the elements as soon as he has received them. There ought to be no legislation about the matter but in Christian freedom each congregation should act in the way which it finds most meaningful.

A variety of custom obtains during the administration of the Sacrament. Selections are sometimes sung by the choir, hymns are played by the organist, or occasionally there is silence. Again, there can be no legislation about the matter, but we can strongly suggest that whatever is done ought not to distract the worshiper from the sacramental action. If music is to be used, it should not be obtrusive or call attention to itself.

Although we in the Reformed Church have almost universally adopted the Presbyterian custom of receiving communion seated in the pews, we may remind ourselves at this point of our original practice. In the Dutch tradition the Sacrament was received seated at long tables placed either across the front of the church or in the aisles. In the German tradition, from which a number of our congregations come, it was received standing in a semi-circle around the Lord's Table. Once more the principle must be one of freedom but it is good to know that we have the freedom to employ a variety of customs, particularly in special situations, as on the Thursday in Holy Week, which seems to call for another practice.

When all have received the Sacrament, the minister, standing in his place behind the Table, will lead in the saying of Psalm 103, which with the additional verses from Romans, has served as the Post-Communion Thanksgiving in our tradition from the very beginning. The Intercessions which follow should be offered from the same place at the Table. The forms which are given here are only suggstions, but the indicated use of silence is strongly recommended.

After the singing of the final hymn, which should be one of thanksgiving and joy, and the covering of the Table, where that is the custom, the minister pronounces the benediction from some place behind the Table. It is not necessary for him to return to the pulpit for this final word. Especially at Celebrations of the Lord's Supper he should not make his way to the back of the church during the final hymn and pronounce the benediction from there. His presence at the Table for this final invocation of the presence of Christ with his people is an important symbol which ought not to be discarded for reasons of mere practical convenience.

— Howard G. Hageman

Chapter V

LITURGY AND MUSIC

The use of music with The Liturgy and Psalms

Music in the worship service, whether it is by the congregation, the choir, the organist, or the soloist, should be the servant of the liturgy. It should be functional in that its purpose and use is to help carry the thrust of each section of the service to its culmination and conclusion. It should also help carry out the general theme of the worship and thus serve as a unifying force. In this latter sense it can function as a powerful adjunct to the spoken word. Historically, the Reformed Church has used congregational singing of psalms, hymns and a few sung responses for the main body of its music. It has also used instrumental organ music extensively as well as some choral music. However, the congregational hymn remains the primary source of its sung music. The chief aim and purpose of choir and organ music is to help lead the congregation in its praise — the singing of hymns, psalms, canticles and liturgical responses. If the main emphasis is shifted from congregational music to that of choir and organ music, the Protestant use of music is changed from its original intent. Therefore, continued effort must be made to retain enthusiastic congregational singing of hymns and liturgical responses, with choir and organ music serving only as aids in this area. Congregational participation in praise of God is vital to retaining the spirit and purpose of worship regained by the people at the time of the Reformation.

Hymns and psalms constitute the main body of sacred song for the congregation. The order of service of the *Liturgy* suggests an opening hymn of praise. This can follow the votum or precede it if the hymn is used as a processional for the choir and clergy. The opening hymn can also be in keeping with the season of the church year or special festive days such as Easter, Christmas, Pentecost and others. The closing hymn can suggest

44

by its text the movement from corporate worship back to the individual lives and work of the people. The hymn "Come, Labor On" is an example of this idea. The closing hymn can also, if carefully chosen, help sum up the main theme of the entire service.

The *Liturgy* suggests using either a hymn or anthem after the congregational statement of the creed, before the sermon. If a hymn is used at this point, it should be directly related to the Scripture lessons, the creed, or the main theme of the day. The middle hymn could be of a more introspective and meditative type, and could lead into the sermon which follows by helping augment the mood and tone of the lessons and sermon.

The selection of hymns for each service should be done with great care as to their appropriateness and effectiveness in each section of the worship. It is as necessary for all the people to participate in singing hymns as for all to join in congregational prayers and responses, for it is the people's main opportunity to respond to God's message to His church.

Sung congregational responses:

The congregation and choir can sing at least three responses in the regular weekly service: the Kyrie Eleison (Lord, have mercy), the Gloria Patri (Glory be to the Father), and the Doxology (Praise God from whom all blessings flow). The Kyrie is a penitential response which appropriately follows the prayer of confession. Nos. 570 or 571 of *The Hymnbook* are available and should be sung in unison by all the people and choir. No. 570 is usually the response more easily sung by all.

The second response suggested is the Gloria Patri following the responsive reading of psalmody. The early Christian Church used this as the final stanza when chanting a psalm, in order to bring the Old Testament psalm into the realm of the New Testament and the Christian Church. This tradition has continued to the present time and its practice is highly recommended in all Christian churches. In the present *Liturgy* the Gloria Patri also climaxes the first part of the service — "The Approach to God" — and is usually sung by all the people as they stand.

The third sung congregational response uses the newer Doxology written by Bishop Thomas Ken of late 17th century

England – "Praise God from whom all blessings flow." Most Protestant churches use this as the climax to the giving of ourselves, our money and our praise in the offertory. It also should be sung "heartily" and with great joy and vigor. Many churches enjoy using the irregular rhythm for the tune from the *Genevan Psalter* as is used in the hymn "All People That on Earth Do Dwell," but *The Hymnbook* uses the tune with straight rhythm in No. 544.

All three responses have had wide historical usage especially in Protestant churches. The Kyrie Eleison is from the Greek language, but singing it in English is highly recommended. The Gloria Patri (not to be confused with the Gloria in Excelsis) is from the Latin and was invariably found as the last verse of chanted psalms. It is classified as a Doxology and is scriptural in content. The Doxology "Praise God from whom all blessings flow" was written in English and has had great and continued popularity in *all* Protestant churches mainly as the climax to the offertory.

Choir music in the church service:

Choir and organ music also serve important additional functions in the service aside from helping to lead the congregation in its praise. However, these additional uses are subordinate to their primary job. Choir (choral) music can be substituted for congregational hymns at the peril of losing the very thing which the Church has worked so hard to retain at various times in its history – the congregation's song. Periodically the Church has had to wrest its music back from the professional religious class of monks and clergy as well as from the professional singer and leader and give it to the people. If choirs represent the congregation and not the clergy, the balance is perhaps more easily kept. If not, the professional – both clergy and choir – will again take over too much and the layman will retain little participation in the entire service. If the clergy, the organist, the choir and the lay congregation understand their parts in the service and their functions in the liturgy, all are apt to retain a better balance of responsibility for action. The choir and organ personnel should assume the role of both artistic leader and servant to the congregation in order to achieve a good relationship. There are times when the choir can speak out as an individual unit and enhance or help carry out the service. Anthems can be extensions of the Word, commentaries on the action and meaning of the Word, as well as high praise, exaltation, and prayer. If the text and music are closely related to the Scripture lessons, an anthem can serve as an artistic link between the two. A suitable anthem could serve well after the Scripture lessons or after the creed as a fine bridge which ends the statement of faith and leads into the sermon. A general criterion to follow should be that the anthem serve some function and not be merely a fancy addition to the service as "special music". In most cases, choral music serves better than instrumental since it contains — or should contain — a meaningful text. It is recommended that the text of the anthem be printed in the bulletin for the service so that it can be read as a poem, a prose selection, or as a direct piece of Scripture. The music to which the text is set will be more effective if the words are understood and seen as an entire work, as well as heard phrase by phrase in the singing. An overly fancy, pretentious anthem sung badly can be, as Dr. Coffin said, "a serious menace to common worship." (p. 117, *The Public Worship of God*, The Westminster Press) a well-chosen anthem sung sincerely and effectively can "lend wings to theology" and help stimulate fervor and depth of feeling which the spoken word might not always be able to do alone.

Another excellent place for using an anthem in a semi-liturgical function is during the offertory. The offering is both a giving of our lives and a portion of our substance in response to God's message to us through the lessons and the sermon which preceded it. At this time the church, as God's people, gives itself in renewal and gratefulness for its redemption. The music of the offertory can also be a giving of artistic work either in organ selections, improvisation, choir anthems or solos. We, the people of God, give our lives, our money and our highest artistic expression of love and thankfulness during the offertory. The gathering of the offering, the singing of the choir and the commitment of each individual can occur simultaneously, and all can be climaxed in a great expression of thankfulness when all sing the "Praise God" at the conclusion of the offertory.

Besides anthems, choirs can sing introits, responses to prayers and short responses to the benediction. Introits sung after the organ prelude and before the votum can be an effective introduction to the official opening of the service. They can be praise and thanks for the new day, for the opportunity for corporate worship, or they can be a call to worship. They can also relate to the special theme of the day or relate to the special day itself, such as Easter. They should be reasonably short and should not be in lieu of the votum which is the prerogative of the clergy. Occasionally the introit could be a choral rendition of the chorale or hymn tune which was the basis for the organist's prelude. In general, the introit is not at all necessary to the service but could be a significant aid in setting the tone of the worship service which follows it. Choral responses to prayers and benedictions are also possible but again not necessary. It is not in the official realm of the choir to sing a benediction as this also comes from the office of the ordained minister. Neither is it a good time for the choir to sing a short anthem. After the congregation has been officially dismissed with the benediction, it should be on its way with dispatch and rejoicing.

Organ music in the church service:

Competent organists are usually trained in taste as well as in technique. However, their repertory of preludes and postludes should strive to contain music in a style worthy of the particular congregations they serve. Preludes need not be brilliant, half-length recitals, nor do they need to be "mood music" and sentimental trivia. They, of course, can and should be closely related to the type of service which is to follow. If no vocal music is used for the offertory, organ music is used. No type of music can or should be prescribed except that the organist must be aware that the offertory is an integral part of the liturgy and is not an added vehicle to enhance the reputation of the performer. Organist and choir members can make their musical offering while the congregation makes its commitment. At the close of the offertory all forces join in the climax — the Doxology.

The main function of organ music is to help lead God's people in corporate worship through sacred songs and psalms. The organist's main job is to play hymns well, so that the congregation will sing them well. He should try to help lead their singing by phrasing with them, stimulating their efforts, and at the same time learn to sense the pulse of the congregation. This is his main task and perhaps his most difficult one. He must also sense the various styles and tempi of the many different kinds of hymns and hymn tunes. Organ music can help or hinder a service as much as any other single item; therefore the organist must be in full accord with the leader (the minister) as to how the service is to go. Clergy, organists and choir directors plan well in advance so that each service may be a powerful worship with music fulfilling its proper function.

Additional music for the communion service:

Aside from the standard Kyrie, Gloria Patri and the Doxology, many church choirs sing the Sanctus which occurs during the communion prayer of the liturgy. It is not mandatory that it be sung or even chanted and is perhaps as well *said* by the officiant. The Sanctus and Benedictus, however, have been sung parts of communion before as well as after the Reformation. Nos. 581, 582, 583 and 584 in *The Hymnbook* are settings of the Sanctus. The Sanctus and Benedictus are on page 66 of the *Liturgy and Psalms* under the rubric "Here may be said or sung." It is regrettable that there is no simple setting of the Benedictus (Blessed is he that cometh in the name of the Lord) for choir or congregational singing. The Sanctus, from Isaiah, is liturgically symbolic of the heavenly song (the choir) while the Benedictus is from Christ's entry into Jerusalem and is symbolic of the people's song. Therefore the Sanctus and Benedictus are the heavenly and earthly song. Perhaps it would be liturgically effective if the entire congregation recited it in unison after the choir's singing of the Sanctus. It would be even more effective if the people were to sing it to some straight-forward tune or chant. The communion prayer continues after these two canticles.

During communion or the passing of the elements, most churches use organ music of familiar hymn tunes. Some organists play unfamiliar music of a more mystical character which allows the people to do their own meditations and prayers. Others play quiet, tasteful improvisations on hymn tunes. In some churches

the ministers read Scripture or short meditations. Still other
communion services use complete silence while the congregation
prays and partakes. Silence can be very telling once the congregation becomes accustomed to it and does not feel uncom-
fortable. Music can help if it is not crude, too loud, or banal.
Again, it could be "a menace to common worship." Choral music
can be effective during communion by using hymns, chants, or
anthems. Liturgically, the service of the Eucharist was meant
to be a thanksgiving service in the early church, but it has
gradually assumed the remembrance of the passion of our Lord
and has rather neglected the Easter aspect with its accompany-
ing thanksgiving for redemption. The music for communion
should not be morbidly concerned with death, but should also
relate the resurrection and its reverently happy aspect.

Music itself is not worship, but it can be worshipful. Just as
we do not worship the Word or the preacher who proclaims it,
so we do not worship music or the musician. We worship the
God whom the music celebrates in many different styles and
media. The attitude towards music in Christian worship is not
the same as in a concert hall where it is performed for music's
sake and the enjoyment of the audience. Music in the worship
service exists for God's sake and as an aid to the worshipping
congregation.

— Laurence Grooters

Chapter VI

LITURGY AND CEREMONIAL

It is nearly impossible to write anything authoritative or definitive about the ceremonial of the Reformed Church or about the ornamentation of its churches or the vestments of its ministers. A negative attitude towards all of them is a consistent strain in Reformed piety from the Sixteenth Century onwards, and the vestiges of them that we can find vary so greatly from place to place and from time to time that very little can be asserted that cannot be contradicted by another investigator.

Almost from the first, many Reformed Churches looked upon the Mass as something to be abolished. By the fifteen-sixties the Elector Frederick the Pious of the Palatine could insert in his Heidelberg Catechism the famous description of the Mass an "an idolatry to be condemned," and no one in the Reformed Church would have thought of contradicting him. With the abolition of the Mass came quite naturally the abolition of all of its shadowy ceremonies, including the sacred vestments of the ministers and the holy array of the sanctuary.

If the Reformed worship were to have any outward beauty at all, it should be the "beauty of holiness" (Psalm 96:9) shining from the faces and persons of the members of the assembly. If it were to have any form or comeliness, it should be no other than, "He has commanded in His Word" (H. C. 96). If it were to have any rubrics at all, it should find them in the admonition of Paul (I Cor. 14:50), "Let all things be done decently and in order."

With the dissolution of older traditions here in America, however, we find many departures from these basic principles in conservative as well as in liberal circles. Some have been attracted to the informality of neighboring groups and have substituted that for the simplicity of old. They are not the same. Simple Calvinistic worship was filled with the kind of formality

51

that surely is appropriate when people enter into the presence of their King.

Others have borrowed from churches with another liturgical tradition, much ecclesiastical furniture, and millinery designed to improve upon the "barrenness" of the old Reformed service. In doing so, they often adopted things that are out of place in our circles completely and instituted ceremonies and practices which are meaningless and even a bit ridiculous.

It is the object of this chapter, therefore, to make suggestions which hopefully may keep our churches from going too far from Reformed principles in either direction.

Vestments

There is general agreement that at the time of the Reformation, ministers began to preach in their street dress or in academic dress in the Reformed churches. Since at the time most occupations and professions had their own distinctive costume, ministers were nearly aways clearly identifiable as such from their clothing. The vestments of the medieval clergy, with their symbolic meaning, were simply done away with.

In time, however, as fashions changed, the older clerical dress was retained on formal occasions (including, of course, public worship), while other kinds of clothing were used every day. Hence, in nearly every historic national Reformed Church, a clerical dress for use in official functions re-appeared. It takes widely different forms in different lands, from the wide flowing "palast" of Hungarian Reformed ministers to the buttoned "talar" with turned down collar of German and German-Swiss pastors to the Calvin or Geneva robe of French and Dutch Reformed ministers to the gown and bands of the Scottish Presbyterian clergy.

During the Nineteenth Century when the "free church" movement caused separations from the ancient "state" Reformed Churches of Europe, the separatists usually left off the clerical robes once again and returned to the practice of wearing street dress (usually black) into the pulpit. This practice spread among all the Reformed Churches in America.

There is ample precedent, therefore, for both current practices: an official robe of office or a plain, dark suit of more or less current fashion. Ministers should not go beyond one of these, however. The use of stoles, (essentially a vestment of the Mass), pectoral crosses, or other such items in church services exceeds the rule of simplicity, calls attention to the wearer and ought to be avoided.

The only other people who customarily wear vestments of any sort in Reformed Churches are the choir members. Churches should insist on simplicity and oppose all ostentation in choir robes as well as in ministerial dress.

Ceremonial

In the ordinary Sunday services of the Reformed Church very little ceremony is contemplated. The minister stands quietly in the pulpit (or at the Lord's Table as suggested in other chapters) and does nothing to call attention to himself. If he must take the offering plates from the ushers, let him do so in the simplest the most convenient way. Only when he pronounces the benediction and salutation does he add any ceremonial action, and that is the Scriptural one of the lifting of the hands. The minister is not a showy master of ceremonies, but a humble ambassador of the great King. Let him keep this always in mind.

When baptism is administered, the minister must go to the place appointed and apply the water to the head of the child or persons to be baptized. He should do this with his hand (or from a small pitcher, where this is provided) once or three times, without any further ceremony. It does not seem necessary to take the child from the parent's into his own arms.

At the Lord's Table the ceremony of taking and breaking the bread and taking the cup into the hands is to be observed. When the original practice of the Reformed churches was still retained and the people came and sat or stood around the Lord's Table, this was a necessary and highly practical action. In most cases today, it is symbolic, but it has an appropriate place in our service, nevertheless. In addition, where a flagon and chalice are still provided, the minister may pour the wine into the chalice before taking it into his hand.

At ordinations, marriages, and at the admission of baptized persons to the Lord's Table, the ceremony of kneeling for a blessing is a good one. Kneeling was once common in Reformed Churches whenever prayer was offered. Gradually, however, and possibly because of its vivid association in the minds of the early generations with Roman Catholic adoration of the host, it fell into disuse in public worship. In many continental Reformed Churches the people stand for prayer. In the Netherlands it was customary for a while for the men to stand while the women remained seated. In the United States most churches have conformed to the general Protestant practice of remaining seated during the prayers of the church, although the congregation usually stands for the brief opening prayers and for the benediction at the end of the service. Where kneeling is still indicated, as in the services mentioned above, it should be on both knees with the body erect (not hunched down) and a kneeler or pillow provided. The blessing may be given by the laying on of (one or both) hands or merely by extending the hands over the person receiving the benediction. This is a beautiful and Scriptural practice which ought to be more common among us than it is.

There seems to be no particular need to introduce other, additional ceremonies into our public worship. To make a ceremony of the lighting and snuffing of candles, or the opening of the Bible, or of any other accompaniments of the church services is surely not appropriate in the Reformed Church. Those who adhere to the rule of simplicity will have public worship that is solemn and majestic as well as beautiful and pure.

Ornaments

Many Reformed Churches of the present have departed furthest from the landmarks of the fathers in the matter of the decoration and ornamentation of their buildings and their furnishings. Although whitewashed walls and rough, ugly appointments were not the preference of former generations at all, as the legends of today would lead us to believe, neither were pictures, crosses, ceremonial candles and other paraphernalia of that sort ever contemplated for our church buildings. In this respect, too, the simplicity of Biblical piety brought with it its own beauty and reverent spirit.

For better or worse, however, we now have a good deal of ornamentation in our churches which ought to be properly used rather than abused.

The only ornamentation required for the Lord's Table is the linen tablecloth for Communion and the lesser cloths or napkins with which the elements are covered. In many places, however, a permanent table covering has been provided. It is perfectly proper to use the same cover throughout the year. If several coverings in the so-called "liturgical colors" are available, the following simple rule for their use may be helpful:

> Purple — Season of Advent; Ninth Sunday before Easter to Good Friday; a Day of Humiliation and Prayer.
>
> White — Season of Christmas and First Sunday after Epiphany; Season of Easter; Pentecost, and the Sunday after Pentecost, and Reformation Day.
>
> Green — The other Sundays after Epiphany; the other Sundays after Pentecost; a Day of General Thanksgiving.
>
> Red may be used, if available, for Pentecost, Reformation Day and anniversaries of the local congregation. Black is often used on Good Friday.

There are many variations of this sequence to be found. Pulpit and lectern antependia will naturally agree in color with the coverings of the Lord's Table.

Where a cross and candlesticks have not been provided for the Lord's Table, it is advisable not to do so. They do not belong to our tradition and are being replaced in many other churches where their use was formerly universal. In some Reformed circles where the cross was a symbol of persecution and perversion to Roman Catholicism, there is a distinct prejudice against its use anywhere in the church. Hungarian Reformed churches, for example, have substituted the rooster and the star for the cross on their steeples for this very reason. In most cases, however, a single use of the cross on the chancel wall, for example, can hardly be faulted.

There is some question about what, if anything, should be placed on the Lord's Table on Sundays when there is no Communion. Some feel that the offering plates and flowers have no place there and should be located on stands elsewhere. Lately there has been an increasing tendency to place an open Bible or one or more Communion vessels on the Table regularly. Perhaps it would be best to place nothing on it at all.

The use of pictures on the walls or in the windows of Reformed Churches is an innovation which has had some unfortunate results. Many people believe that these pictures really show us what Christ and the apostles looked like, and they have been the victims of many misapprehensions because this is a race-conscious age. We would do well to avoid future use of pictures and picture-windows and go back to the older practice of designs, non-pictorial symbols or Scripture texts as the sole subjects of wall and window decorations.

Flags, banners and plaques are also frequently found in the churches. They should be appropriate and not too numerous, large or ostentatious.

Church decorations for Christmas, Easter, Mother's Day or Children's Day seem to have been borrowed from secular practice more than from any particular religious sentiment. When they are limited in number and cost, and do not require the moving or replacement of the pulpit, the Lord's Table or the baptismal font, which speak to us of the essential ministry of the Word and Sacraments, they cannot be rejected. It may well be asked why the Festival of Pentecost is not also honored with some special decoration of the church.

Conclusion

Liturgical worship has little or nothing to do with ceremonialism and ornamentation. Reformed liturgical worship is at its best when ecclesiastical fussiness and illegitimate imitation are kept at a minimum. "Let all things be done decently and in order!"

— Charles W. Krahe, Jr.

Chapter VII

LITURGY AND ARCHITECTURE

The Use of *The Liturgy* Within the Architectural Disposition of the Local Church.

The purpose of this paper is to offer a rationale for the use of "The Order of Worship" (as outlined on pages 5 and 6 of *The Liturgy,* and which follow in full form on subsequent pages) within the architectural situation presented by the local church. Because of the variety of architectural placement for the pulpit, font, and table within our Reformed churches, consideration will be given to an ideal situation in which the architecture is commensurate with the liturgy, followed by consideration of such situations where other types of architecture will force necessary variants upon the liturgy.

This paper will not try to argue for "what should be" in terms of architecture. The General Synod in 1966 (GSM 1966, p. 205) through its Theological Commission spoke to the issue of architecture for Reformed churches by its hearty endorsement and commendation of *CHRIST AND ARCHITECTURE, building Presbyterian/Reformed churches,* by Donald J. Bruggink and Carl H. Droppers (Grand Rapids: Eerdmans, 1965). The arguments of that volume will not be repeated here.

The celebration of the liturgy within the Reformed architectural context:

The Reformed architectural context is one in which the architecture augments worship as understood within the Reformed tradition. The pulpit will have a prominent place, and by its size, shape and position will make its indispensability plain. The font will be visible to the congregation and enable baptism to be celebrated in the midst of the body of Christ. The table will be prominent, giving such emphasis to the sacrament of the

57

Lord's Supper as befits the Eucharistic feast of our Lord. Since most of our congregations have never completed the Reformation desired by Calvin, that the church should return to the New Testament practice of a weekly celebration, it is all the more necessary that the table be a weekly reminder of the sacrament.

Within a Reformed architectural context it will be possible for the minister to move easily between pulpit, font and table, always able to be seen and heard by the congregation.

The Approach to God:

"The Approach to God" (*Liturgy*, p. 5), may be conducted from behind the Lord's table, facing the congregation. By beginning the service in this way, the minister clarifies liturgically our theological understanding of our approach to God. The minister's position at the table witnesses to the awareness that we come to God only through Christ the redeemer. While it is certainly true that from the pulpit we proclaim the Christ, nonetheless the forceful way in which the table reminds us of Christ's atoning sacrifice makes it a particularly fitting place from which to begin worship. If there is a presbyters' (elders') bench behind the table, it is appropriate for the minister to sit there while waiting for the service to begin.

The position of the minister at the Lord's table for "The Approach to God" has no less a historical precedent than the practice of John Calvin at Strasbourg.[1] That the practice was abandoned appears to be from practical rather than theological considerations. The great gothic churches made it difficult to be heard when standing in the open at the Lord's table apart from the sounding board of the pulpit,[2] and the antipathy for the Mass which had resulted in the demolition of the stone altars had led some churches to erect temporary tables only upon the occasion of the celebration of the sacrament. In such churches, which were left with a pulpit as their only piece of liturgical furniture, the entire service was of necessity conducted therefrom. In our day when amplification systems solve our accoustical problems and our churches no longer fear the impli-

[1]W. D. Maxwell, *John Knox's Genevan Service Book, 1556* (Edinburgh: Oliver & Boyd, 1931), pp. 36ff.
[2]*Ibid*, p. 38.

cations of the Mass through the presence of a table, we can again return to the good practice of John Calvin to approach God at the table of our Lord.

The Word of God:

With the singing of the Gloria Patri, the minister should ascend into the pulpit for the prayer of illumination, Scripture, sermon and prayer of blessing on the Word. It is unfortunate that contrary to the practice of the early Reformed churches a hymn should separate the Scripture from the sermon. The movement from the table to the pulpit gives emphasis to the importance of the proclamation of God's word.

The Response to the Word:

> In defining the indispensable elements of Christian worship, Calvin appealed to the "invariable custom" of the early church. "No assembly of the Church should be held," he asserted, "without the word being preached, prayers offered, the Lord's supper administered, and alms given."[3]

Unfortunately, the abuse of the Lord's Supper in the Middle Ages had turned it into a daily Mass for the priest, and a yearly participation for the faithful. The less faithful were difficult to get to the communion even once a year. When the Reformers wanted to restore the order of worship to the "invariable custom of the early church" by a weekly celebration of the sacrament, it was the civil magistrates (who usually controlled the church in Reformed cities and lands) who rejected the proposal in favor of a quarterly celebration. When the Synod of Dort met, establishing not only their famous canons, but also a complete church order, they recognized the insufficiency of quarterly communion, but were content to decree that the Lord's Supper should be celebrated "not less than four times a year, for the time being," the latter phrase clearly looking forward to a more frequent celebration.

In most of our Reformed churches we still fall far short of the

[3]Nichols, James Hastings, CORPORATE WORSHIP IN THE REFORMED TRADITION (Philadelphia: The Westminster Press, 1968), p. 29, quoting Calvin, *Institutes* 4:17:44.

reformation of worship envisioned by such worthies as John Calvin, Peter Martyr, and Martin Bucer. Our service is still truncated as can be clearly seen by comparing the outlines on page 5 of our *Liturgy*. A very minimal gesture which can be made in the direction of a return to a greater emphasis upon the Lord's Supper is to leave the pulpit and go to the table to conduct "The Response to the Word". It should be understood that in its fullest sense the response to the Word of God is to come to the Eucharistic table to partake in faith of Christ, the Lamb of God who takes away the sins of the world. Even when the sacrament is not celebrated our response should still take us to the table in recognition of what should fittingly be the climax of worship on the day of resurrection. It is fitting that the entire "Response to God" should be performed at the table.

The offering represents a considerable liturgical problem. Originally the offering was the bringing of bread and wine for the supper so that there would be something to eat and drink. Alms were collected separately. At the time of the Reformation Archbishop Cranmer of the Church of England substituted the collection of alms, or offerings, for the traditional offertory of bread and wine for the supper. However, in the Reformed churches of the continent, it was customary to have the alms boxes at the door of the church where one could leave one's offering of money when leaving the church.

What should we do with our offerings of money, and when should we collect them? To the last part of the question your committee is in agreement with the liturgy of the Reformed Church. The reception of the offering of money during "The Response to the Word" is appropriate insofar as our gifts are tokens of lives dedicated to God in response to His word.

To the question of where to place the offering there is no single answer. Some feel, with Cranmer, that the offering of money takes the place of the bringing of bread and wine to the Lord's table by the congregation, and that therefore, the money can appropriately be placed on the table. Others, following an interpretation to come out of the Cambridge Ecclesiology of the last century, feel that the placing of our offerings of money on the table is an appropriate symbol of the giving of our lives as a sacrifice to God.

Others, governed by theological considerations, feel that it is desirable that the offerings of money not be placed on the table lest the nature of the sacrament as a sign of God's grace be confused. When we celebrate the sacrament, it is to come to Christ to receive forgiveness and life in participation in the death and resurrection of Christ. The sacrament is in no sense a celebration of what we bring to God but rather of what He has done for us — His grace in Christ. Thus it would seem more appropriate that the plates be placed on a small shelf or table provided for that purpose. Within our liturgy we should maintain the crucial Reformation distinction between what we offer and the celebration of what God has offered on our behalf, by placing our gifts elsewhere than upon the Lord's table.

When the Lord's Supper is celebrated it is fitting for the presbyters to sit with the ministers on the presbyters' bench behind the table, or on chairs set about the table. Best of all is an architectural setting where the Reformed practice of the entire communicant congregation sitting about the table can be exercised. In that instance the people will remain in their pews until the words of consecration (pp. 67-68). Then, beginning at either the front or the back of the church, the people will move forward to the table. After sitting (or standing if sitting is not possible), the minister will speak a summary of the words of consecration (p. 68) to each group of communicants as they are seated at the table. A short benediction will follow and the people will raise and return to their pews while another group of the congregation comes forward. After the last group have partaken and returned to their pews the Psalm of Thanksgiving (pp. 68-69) will be said by all. If the congregation is so fortunate as to have a table large enough to accommodate all of the communicants at one sitting, then it would be appropriate to include the Communion Thanksgiving at the table as well.

The Liturgy in Other Architectural Settings:

During the last half of the Nineteenth Century a type of church architecture became so pervasive that it could be called "American traditional". It reflected the tremendous influence of the itinerant evangelist who often preached in public halls, using the stage for his pulpit and the choral gallery behind the stage for his choir. The competition offered by the itinerant evangelist influenced the church to introduce architectural features which mimicked the arrangements of the secular concert hall. Churches began to have stages with reading desks instead of pulpits, and instead of a choir behind the rest of the congregation to assist them in praise, it became as well a means of entertainment (witness the oft used term "special music"). The result of these changes was that the table assumed a very minor role in the sanctuary, usually being relegated to a spot on the floor immediately in front of the pulpit where it served as a repository for flowers and offering plates. Most of us have grown up in these "American traditional" churches and in many instances it is necessary that the architectural arrangements remain as they are. Within these circumstances it is practical to begin "The Approach to God" at the table only if there is ordinarily enough room behind it to stand and face the congregation. If this is not the case, then the entire service, including "The Response to the Word" will of necessity be taken from the pulpit.

The Split Chancel:

The Cambridge Ecclesiologists of the Oxford Movement began their popularization of this romanticized medieval architecture in the middle of the nineteenth century. Its arrangements are familiar to most of us. The chancel is split with a lectern on one side and a pulpit on the other. Behind them is the choir, facing one another across a wide, open space which allows an unobstructed view by the congregation of the communion table, fixed to the east wall of the chancel, which is the focal point of attention.

Where possible, the table should be moved forward, as close as possible to the people. (In Roman Catholic Churches altars against the east wall where the priest has to celebrate with his back to the people are no longer tolerated. All Roman churches have been ordered to procure permanent tables of fitting beauty and craftsmanship to stand as close to the congregation as possible, where the Supper may be celebrated with the priest facing the people. It would be a strange travesty if in our day

Reformed Churches should prove to be less reformed than the Church of Rome). When the table has been so moved, the consistory may wish to fill the empty space against the east well with a presbyters' bench. Such were used by some of the early Reformed Churches (e.g., Farel's church in Neuchatel). "The Approach to God" as well as "The Response to the Word" should be conducted from behind the table.

Even in a church with a split chancel, "The Word of God," including the reading of Scripture, will be done from the pulpit. In this type of church in particular, it is all the more desirable not to confuse the table with the reception of monetary gifts. It should also be noted that whatever is to be done with the offering, the chancel area is not the inviolate preserve of the minister. Elders, deacons, and children from the Sunday School have as much right to enter the chancel to bring the offering as does the minister to be there. It should not be necessary for the minister to handle the offering as those appointed to its reception are generally capable of putting it in its proper place.

It is perhaps unnecessary to emphasize that the Lord's Supper must be celebrated from behind the Lord's table, facing the people, and that this should be the position for the final portion of the service when the sacrament is not celebrated.

Epilogue

The above suggestions should not be understood to be "necessities of the faith". Meaningful worship can be conducted without them. Nor should they be looked upon as legalistic requirements which must be followed to be in good and proper standing with the brethren. While being offered neither as necessary to salvation nor as legal requirements, they should be taken for what they are, suggestions for a meaningful way of ordering our worship of God. They have the commendation of many of the great leaders of the Reformation churches, as well as having several centuries of usage behind them — albeit our American experience has often served to cut us off from our rightful heritage as Reformed.

A rightly ordered worship should never be looked upon as a substitute for a clearly spoken message from God's Word. But, what we see and what we do have a powerful effect on forming our lives, and it is therefore desirable that what we see architecturally and hear liturgically, and what we do in our acts of worship, be in accordance with the faith, reformed according to the Word of God, to which we are committed.

— Donald J. Bruggink

Chapter VIII

THE MARRIAGE SERVICE

The wedding ceremony is probably the best known part of the liturgy, even among those who seldom attend other church services. Most people get married, and most others at least attend a wedding occasionally: so that includes just about everybody. People who seldom if ever enter a church on other occasions are usually glad to go for a wedding. Indeed, in a secular world, the feeling is still pretty generally prevalent that the place for a wedding is in the church. This presents both an opportunity and a danger: opportunity because an occasion is provided for the clear statement of Christian love which undergirds the ceremony at a time when people are most susceptible to it; and danger because it is all too easy for the sacred nature of the ceremony to be subverted and lost in a fashion parade.

The wedding, like any other service in the church, is a sacred ceremony directed to the praise and glory of God. This must be kept foremost in the minds of the minister who presides and the bridal couple who have come to exchange their vows. Before the use of the church is granted, and the services of the minister are engaged, a conference should be held in which this is clearly spelled out. Persons who do not worship God in the church, and have no intention of doing so, should not be married in the church. What can words such as those likening marriage "to the mystical union which exists between Christ and His Church" possibly mean to those who are not in any way part of the Body of Christ? For those who do not wish to be married in Christian bonds, there are civic officials who are duly authorized to witness and solemnize their vows for them. If coming to the church is purely a matter of sentiment, or the wish to have a traditional setting for a fashionable display of wedding garments, they should be informed at once that the church is not the place for their wedding.

Before sending the couple elsewhere, however, the minister

65

should seek to take full advantage of the exceptional opportunity he has to bring them to a knowledge of God, and to show them the unique nature of Christian love. Society as a whole is well aware of the difference between infatuation with temporary states of mind, whether of sex or soppy sentiment, and the more enduring qualities which lead to devotion that abides "for better, for worse, for richer, for poorer, in sickness and in health, to love and to cherish, till death us do part, according to God's holy ordinance." It is a rare couple indeed who will not respond positively and in gratitude to the offer of assistance in launching the high venture of matrimony on such a firm foundation. This means, of course, that the minister must be prepared to spend long hours in pre-marital counselling, which may even include a course in the fundamentals of the Christian religion. But most couples are quite ready at the time of their marriage to receive such instruction, especially if it is connected with a sound study of the many new situations which will confront them in the married state.[1] There is no finer opportunity for evangelism in the finest sense of the word than that provided by the young couple who are about to form a new family unit. The sympathetic and skillful pastor who will take the time to make every word of the marriage ceremony stand out in its full meaning, and then celebrate this joyful occasion in all its grandeur by leading the bride and groom step by step through each phrase and prayer is communicating the Gospel of Jesus Christ to them and to all the guests in a way that can be felt as well as seen and heard. Don't forget how many times our Lord likened the kingdom of heaven to a wedding feast!

Ministers and elders should be well aware of this superlative teaching opportunity provided by a wedding. At the same time they should be on their guard against those who would profane the church by seeking to hire it for the occasion much as they would hire the hall for the reception that follows. There is no reason for the church to spoil the gaity of the reception; but they can enhance it with a deeper level of joy if first they have launched the wedding celebration on the high level of love which the liturgy for marriage expresses.

[1]For information on this subject write to: Family Life Publications, Inc. Durham, North Carolina.

The question has been raised whether or not there should be a ceremony provided for use by ministers with those who do not want a religious service. If the above approach to marriage is valid, it would not seem so. The unique position of the minister as a civil servant for weddings is one that should be used with the utmost discretion. There may be those special occasions when a minister will be called upon to perform a ceremony under circumstances which do not fit all the ideal requirements for a wedding. By that I do not mean when the bride is found to be pregnant. Rather, there will sometimes be marriages in which religious differences are present, and the feelings of those who do not share our views must be respected. It would not be possible to write a ceremony covering all such cases, so the pastor must approach each situation on its own merits. If his attitude is pastoral rather than judgmental, and if he feels that he should not deny the authority of his office to the couple who seek his help, then he should also be able to adapt the service to the need at hand. The marriage service, excellent though it may be, is not a required part of the liturgy as are other services such as baptism, communion and the service of the Lord's Day. This will be true especially when a member of the parish asks the minister to officiate at a wedding with one not of our persuasion, but who nonetheless is determined to go ahead with the wedding no matter what church or parents may say. The situation calls for judgment and tact, exercised in love, even when the minister feels that rashness may have overtaken good judgment. Let him consult with the elders, so that he may have the benefit of their good counsel. Recognizing that human relations and love may already have been strained, the minister may be a reconciling agent on behalf of the church and the love of God. Too many marriage careers have begun on a note of harshness when youthful self-will has asserted itself against parental wishes. There is one word that is always in order: "Beloved, let us love one another, for love is of God, and he who loves is born of God and knows God." (1 John 4:7).

The Procedure

The procession is no more essential to the wedding than is the processional hymn to worship on the Lord's Day. However, since the custom is so widely established, it is well for us to give some thought to the matter. Perhaps the wedding processional has roots that are older than we can trace. The New Testament parable of the ten bridesmaids who slumbered and slept while the groom's company tarried till midnight is an indication of the antiquity of this custom. A torchlight procession through the streets of the village is probably what is referred to. Whether or not this is so, the custom of having friends of the bride and groom escort them to the place of the ceremony is firmly established. For this reason all the participants should rehearse their part so there will be no uncertainty at the hour of the ceremony.

The groom's company should enter the church first and take their places to the right of the holy table or other place designated for the ceremony. The bride's attendants will take their position on the left. This leaves the center for the bride and the groom. If the bride is escorted by her father and is to be given away by him, she should remain at her father's side until he gives her away. As the minister faces the company then, there may be five people immediately before him: the groom's man on the left, the groom, the bride, the father of the bride, and the bride's attendant. Usually, the bridesmaids will be grouped to the left and right of the bridal party, respectively.

The liturgy begins with the Votum. It is becoming increasingly common for guests to be seated during the ceremony. This is a sensible departure from custom which should be encouraged. There are usually grandparents and other elderly folk present for whom standing would be a burden. It is also easier to see when the guests are seated, and it is more comfortable.

The Votum plays an important part in this ceremony. It is interesting to note that in the 1906 edition of the *Liturgy* the marriage office was the only one that began this way. Its importance is enhanced by what follows . . . "We are assembled here in the sight of God." As indicated elsewhere, the Votum in all services of the liturgy declares the real presence of God. The liturgy for marriage, however, has the distinction of saying it in so many words, not once, but twice.

The presence of God is assumed to be as real as that of those who will sign the marriage certificate as official witnesses.

The minister who speaks the liturgy should be so familiar with these words that he speaks them from the heart. To read it is to lose much of the quality of communication. The service becomes a very personal address from minister to congregation, as well as to the bride and groom. Consequently, the minister is a medium of the Word of God whenever he conducts the liturgy, but the opportunity to do so is never greater than when he is performing a wedding ceremony.

Usually the bridal party will remain standing throughout the ceremony. An exception to this rule should be made in the event that a short sermon is given.

As the service progresses the minister will lead the bride and groom through the prayer for blessing and then turn to the groom, who is still standing on his left in the company of the groom's man. The two questions, "Do you take . . ." and "Will you love . . ." are asked before he is allowed to join his bride-to-be. The family of the bride and all the guests are entitled to hear the groom pledge his life-long love and loyalty as a prelude to his receiving his bride. The same two questions are asked of the bride. The drama that is unfolding before us shows two young people stating their willingness to fulfill the exacting conditions of Christian marriage. All this takes place supposedly with the bride on her father's arm and still a member of his household. Only after both young people have stated their firm intent to marry in Christian bonds, does the minister turn to the father and ask, "Who gives this woman in marriage?" Symbol though it is, its meaning should not be lost. The father gives his daughter away only after certain conditions have been met. To be sure, no one would assume that what is implied could be achieved in the few brief moments of the ceremony. What it does, however, is point to an important symbol. When the father gives his daughter away and she is claimed by the groom, we are given a demonstration of the text from Genesis 2:24 and repeated by our Lord in Mark 10:8: "Therefore shall a man leave his father and mother and cleave to his wife, and the two of them shall become one flesh." The father now joins his family in their pew and the new family unit — husband and wife — stand together, the symbol of a new creation.

In a church where the holy table is in the chancel, it is highly significant that the minister lead the young couple up the chancel steps and, accompanied only by the groom's man and the bride's attendant, leave friends and family behind to stand before the holy table and give their vows to one another. Here each takes the other by the hand and says, "I . . . take you (name) to be my wedded wife (husband)." It is this vow, confirmed by the clasped hands, that constitutes the marriage. Quite literally, its significance is the same as that of a hand-shake sealing an agreement. When a ring is given it is but a symbol of what has been accomplished by the vows taken with clasped hands.

The importance of the ring is often over-emphasized. The words from the old ceremony, "With this ring I thee wed," is a hangover of an outmoded theology. It is not with the ring that one weds. For this reason the committee have put in the preferred position the statement, "This ring I give in token of the covenant made this day . . ." To say, "With this ring I thee wed," is to give lip service to a theology foreign to the Reformed understanding of marriage. The ring is not essential. It may accompany the vows as a token, a very important one and of lasting significance, but not of the essence.

The declaration which follows is given by the minister both as an official of the civil government and as a minister of the Word of God. He is a witness to the solemnization of marriage vows, but, more importantly, as a minister of the Word of God, he declares in the words of our Lord Jesus Christ, "What therefore God has joined together let not man put asunder" (Mark 10:9).

The two passages of Scripture which follow are indicative of the meaning of this ceremony, with Christian love at its heart (I Corinthians 13:4). It is agape which is here celebrated — God's love for man. Men are capable of loving one another in this manner only as first they acknowledge they are loved by God, and seek to love one another in Him.

— Garrett C. Roorda